Command the Month @ the Midnight Gate

Anthony O. Akerele

Command the Month @ the Midnight Gate

Anthony O. Akerele

Command the Month @The Midnight Gate

@ June 2011   Anthony O. Akerele
First Edition
ISBN 9780983776000

Published by
Mountain of Fire and Miracles
Ministries Virginia
6621-H Electronic Drive, Springfield, VA 22151
P.O.Box 5002, Springfield, VA 22150

Phone: 703-982-4073

Email: pastor@mfmvirginia.org
www.mfmvirginia.org

We prohibit reproduction in whole or in part without written permission.

Copyright © 2011 Anthony O. Akerele

All rights reserved.

ISBN: 0983776008
ISBN-13: 9780983776000

DEDICATION

This book is dedicated to God the Father, God the Son and God the Holy Spirit and their representatives on earth, my parents and parents-in-the-Lord for the privilege and opportunity of life and life in Christ as a Priest and a King.

CONTENTS

	Acknowledgment	I
1	Chapter 1 Introduction	1
2	Chapter 2: The Gregorian Calendar	21
3	Chapter 3: Who can command the month?	32
4	Chapter 4: A history of the Months and the meanings of their names	56
5	Chapter 5: Command the First Month: January	61
6	Chapter 6: Command the Second Month: February	70
7	Chapter 7: Command the Third Month: March	75
8	Chapter 8: Command the Fourth Month: April	80
9	Chapter 9: Command the Fifth Month: May	89
10	Chapter 10: Command the Sixth Month: June	109
11	Chapter 11: Command the Seventh Month: July	121
12	Chapter 12: Command the Eighth Month: August	136
13	Chapter 13: Command the Ninth Month: September	146
14	Chapter 14: Command the Tenth Month: October	157
15	Chapter 15: Command the Eleventh Month: November	167
16	Chapter 16: Command the Twelfth Month: December	177
	References	190

Anthony O. Akerele

ACKNOWLEDGMENTS

My sincere appreciation to my wonderful wife, Nnenna , who strongly believes there is something new for mankind in this book and encouraged me with her persistence! Thank you sweetheart!.
I acknowledge "Command the Morning", a source of inspiration for this work and of course the author, my boss and Father-in-the-Lord, Dr. Daniel Olukoya, for offering his shoulders to carry me, like the High Priest of the tabernacle carries the whole congregation of Israel on his shoulders. "If I see further than others, it is by standing on the shoulders of Giants". A Giant in the Lord. Thank you sir!
I also acknowledge all who have ever asked the question " When are you going to write a book?" I humbly yield.

CHAPTER 1

INTRODUCTION

Of the sons of Issachar, men who understood the times, with knowledge of what Israel should do,.....1 Chronicles 12:32

Each month of the calendar is peculiar and unique. So is the gate of every month, a midnight gate by western calendar system. The name of the month, the numerical position and ordinal characteristics in the calendar system are very important in advanced spiritual warfare. The Psalmist declaration: "My times are in your hands O Lord!" suggests time could be somewhere else other than in the hands of the Almighty.

Employ these qualities and characteristics to speak by apostolic decrees to every month and the month will begin to yield you your portion.

Each month of the western world calendar system has spiritual characteristics pointing to a definitely idolatrous background and origin. This is not without consequence when it comes to the battle for the control of time. Some spiritual powers are bent on being in control of your time. They claim they have the time dedicated to themselves and can only release it for the use of man in exchange for worship. Command the Month @The Midnight Gate gives you the spiritual tools to take back the control and administration of time that the adversary has arrogated to himself.

This is a practical prayer manual to command the months of the year. The month cannot but be commanded. "Have you ever in your life commanded the morning, And caused the dawn to know its place?" Job 38:12. The morning is an element of time, so also is the month. If you do not command it, someone else will do, to your detriment of course. The cycles of the months are spiritually significant simply because they form a major subdivision of time-reckoning that impinges on human activities. How well you fare in life is a factor of how you handle and deal with time.

"There is time for everything", the wisest man that ever lived declared in scriptures. Doing the right thing at the wrong time is a guarantee for failure. Not knowing how to redeem the time will make one a late comer in the market place of breakthrough. Above all, time can be extraneously manipulated. Joshua commanded the sun to make the time stand still in order to soundly defeat the enemies of God and the sun stood still. Time was made to recede as token of surety of divine intervention in favor of King Hezekiah.

Who is in control of your time may invariably control your life. The battle for the time of man started with the fall of man. ... the devil has gone down to you! He is filled with fury, because he knows that his time is short." Command the month @ the midnight gate, is an attempt to cultivate a kingdom prayer culture that speaks to the problem instead of talking about the problem. A culture that presupposes that everything and everything can be spoken to and should be spoken to. The worlds were framed by words!

Again, this book is a prayer manual. Meaning you cannot but pray as you go through the book. With an open mind, the answers to the prayers of this book will shock many, particularly those who do not believe in the supernatural. Salvation is a miracle. it is supernatural. Prayers will provoke the supernatural.

MIDNIGHT GATE KINGDOM PRAYER CULTURE

Why midnight?
The first mention of the word midnight in scripture is in the book of Exodus and was by the Lord God Almighty himself as He launched the final attack on Egypt. ...." About midnight will I go out into the midst of Egypt: And all the firstborn in the land of Egypt shall die, from the firstborn of Pharaoh that sits upon

his throne, even unto the firstborn of the maidservant that is behind the mill; and all the firstborn of beasts. Exodus 11:4-5

The attack led to the instantaneous release of the Israelites from the land of bondage. It was done by midnight, The midnight gate is a battle gate.

Samson chose the midnight hour to surprise his enemies. Unpleasant and dangerous surprises are orchestrated at midnight. Judges 16:3

Jdg 16:3 And Samson lay till midnight, and arose at midnight, and took the doors of the gate of the city, and the two posts, and went away with them, bar and all, and put them upon his shoulders, and carried them up to the top of a hill that is before Hebron.

Ruth chose the midnight hour to startle Boaz into a marital reality he could neither deny nor refuse. Marital advances that never fail are made in prayer at the midnight hour.

Ruth 3:8 And it came to pass at midnight, that the man was startled, and turned himself: and, behold, a woman lay at his feet.

While men slept the enemy came and sowed tares. The midnight hour is a time of satanic exchange. It is a time that life could be satanically exchanged with death.

1Ki 3:20 And she arose at midnight, and took my son from beside me, while your handmaid slept, and laid it in her bosom, and laid her dead child in my bosom.

The midnight hour is a moment of destiny. A moment of trouble when the mighty can be taken away without much ado. Check Job 34:20

Job 34:20 In a moment shall they die, and the people shall be troubled at midnight, and pass away: and the mighty shall be taken away without a hand.

The Psalmist regard the midnight hour as time to praise God and bring down His presence into your situation.

Psalm 119:62 At midnight I will rise to give thanks unto you because of your righteous judgments.

Midnight is a time of request that will not go unanswered. Spiritual importunity is best displayed at midnight. See the Master of time, Lord Jesus invoke this quality of the midnight in Luke 11:5-8

Luke 11:5 And he said unto them, Which of you shall have a friend, and shall go unto him at midnight, and say unto him, Friend, lend me three loaves;

Luke 11:6 For a friend of mine in his journey has come to me, and I have nothing to set before him?
Luke 11:7 And he from within shall answer and say, Trouble me not: the door is now shut, and my children are with me in bed; I cannot rise and give you.
Luke 11:8 I say unto you, Though he will not rise and give to him, because he is his friend, yet because of his importunity he will rise and give him as many as he needs.

The midnight hour is a time of landmark deliverance "a la Paul and Silas in the prison cell". They perfected the art of midnight praise to provoke God into a landmark deliverance transaction.

Why Gate?
The gate is an accessing point in time and space. A threshold. The gate is a threshold with great spiritual and physical significance and importance. It is a place of altar, meaning a place of sacrifice and covenant and therefore a place of tremendous power. A place of judgment and decision making, of assembly and of celebration, of traffic and of control of traffic, of monitor and record keeping, of trading and of exchange. Whoever controls the gate wields the power of the gate. The midnight gate for these reasons is a highly critical and crucial gate in advanced spiritual warfare.

Gate is a place of judgment

Deuteronomy 22:24 Then you shall bring them both out unto the gate of that city, and you shall stone them with stones so that they die;

Gen 19:1 And there came two angels to Sodom at evening; and Lot sat in the gate of Sodom: and Lot seeing them rose up to meet them; and he bowed himself with his face toward the ground;

Gen 22:17 That in blessing I will bless you, and in multiplying I will multiply your descendants as the stars of the heaven, and as the sand which is upon the seashore; and your descendants shall possess the gate of their enemies;

Place of traffic
Gen 23:18 To Abraham for a possession in the presence of the children of Heth, before all that went in at the gate of his city.

Place of meeting
Gen 34:20 And Hamor and Shechem his son came unto the gate of their city, and spoke with the men of their city, saying,..

The Midnight gate is a battle gate where power change hands. This is the gate of power where destinies are made and also destroyed. Cyclical problems are handed over at this time. It is the period of the night with the most significant impact on destiny of many if not all and therefore the best time to command the day, week, month and year.

Pray at all times. Pray without ceasing. Praying at the midnight gate adds power and efficacy to your prayers.
For uncontested victories, midnight is the time.
For victories that would spoil the enemy, midnight is the time.
For a defeat the enemy would never recover from, midnight is the time.
For a defeat that would make the enemy hand over without a fight, midnight is the time.

The prayers in this manual are best taken with the MFM Prayer Model. (MFM stands for the Mountain of Fire and Miracles Ministries). The model works! This pattern has worked, it is working and will continue to work! What is MFM Prayer Model?

MFM Prayer Model
Newcomers to this deliverance and warfare prayer ministry always ask questions like " why do you repeat your prayers? Why are you always saying "die!" Why are you always shouting? Why are you cursing? The bible says bless them that curse you? Pray for them that despitefully use you! Why use prayer points in prayers?

We will turn to the bible to answer these questions. The MFM prayer style is the prayer model for end time warfare. Prayer points are nothing but apostolic decrees issued by believers who invariably are Priests and Kings (Rev 1:6). And therefore, Job 22: 28 "Thou shalt also decree a thing, and it shall be established unto thee."

The dominion lost in the garden of Eden, has been restored in SALVATION. The regain of dominion is a regain of authority. Ecclesiastes 8: 4 "Where the word of a king is, there is power: and who may say unto him, What doest thou?" Awareness and consciousness of our regained dominion as priests and kings, is made manifest in the MFM prayer model of "prayer by apostolic decrees."

Everybody gathered at the same place at the same time for the same purpose and saying the same prayer the same way unleashes a tremendous power of agreement like the power of "Let US" of Genesis1 during creation. It is an example of power of agreement and also a practice in the use of the power of agreement in prayer. Matthew 18:19 "Again I say unto you, That if two of you shall agree on earth as touching any thing that they shall ask, it shall be done for them of my Father which is in heaven."

The continuous repetition of an apostolic decree until a release by the Spirit, in the MFM prayer model is a Gethsemanic approach to warfare prayers. In the garden of Gethsemane Jesus came back to the disciples and found them sleeping. Matthew 26:44 "And he left them, and went away again, and prayed the third time, **saying the same words.**" That was not a vain repetition. It is also not a vain repetition to continuously declare " I shall not die but live to declare the word of God"

Every profession has a language or lingo. So does spiritual warfare. In Genesis 3, the moment Eve ate of the fruit she died. She was separated immediately from God. Die as used in the MFM prayer model signifies separation. Power of failure at the edge of breakthrough die out of my life!!! means power of failure at the edge of breakthrough be separated from me. Spirits don't die. They can
be however commanded to be separated from us. Evil covenants and evil dedications affecting my life, die! means evil covenants and evil dedications stop affecting my life, be separate from my life.

Luke 6: 28 "Bless them that curse you, and pray for them which despitefully use you." Your blessing of those that curse you was never intended to make them prosper in their wickedness. Otherwise it would be contrary to Psalms 7:9 Oh let the wickedness of the wicked come to an end; but establish the just: for the righteous God trieth the hearts and reins. Whatsoever puts an end to wickedness lawfully is a blessing. James 5:20 "Let him know, that he which converteth the sinner from the error of his way shall save a soul from death, and shall hide a multitude of sins." Whatsoever converts the sinner from the error of his way is the type of blessing referred to by Luke 6:28.The wicked must be stopped in their tracks of wickedness. Take a look at what Apostle Paul did.

6 And when they had gone through the isle unto Paphos, they found a certain sorcerer, a false prophet, a Jew, whose name was Barjesus: 7 Which was with the deputy of the country, Sergius Paulus, a prudent man; who called for Barnabas and Saul, and desired to hear the word of God. 8 But Elymas the sorcerer (for so is his name by interpretation) withstood them, seeking to turn away the deputy from the faith. 9 Then Saul, (who also is called Paul,) filled with the Holy Ghost, set his eyes on him, 10 And said, O full of all subtilty and all mischief, thou child of the devil, thou enemy of all righteousness, wilt thou not cease to pervert the right ways of the Lord? 11 And now, behold, the hand of the Lord is upon thee, and thou shalt be blind, not seeing the sun for a season. And immediately there fell on him a mist and a darkness; and he went about seeking some to lead him by the hand. 12 Then the deputy, when he saw what was done, believed, being astonished at the doctrine of the Lord.
Acts 13:5-12 (KJV)

To turn someone away from faith is to preach rebellion. A sorcerer stands condemned already by scriptures. You are not going to bless who God has cursed. Apostle Paul handled the sorcerer showing how a sorcerer, an enemy of God, should be handled.

This is the scriptural basis of the MFM prayer model for end-time warfare and deliverance.

This is the prescribed model for the decrees in this prayer manual.
Shall we war!!!

The following decrees are to be taken starting at least thirty minutes before midnight and at least thirty minutes to one hour after midnight on the last day to the first day of the month.

As a Priest and a King in Christ, with the sacrifice of Christ, I stand at the midnight gate to decree:

- On the sacrifice of Christ and the glory of the living God I lay the foundation of the new month for divine worship, divine fellowship and divine communion...For dominion, prosperity, good health and success, in the name of Jesus.

- I tender the sacrifice of Christ to undo every evil dedication of the month and I rededicate the month to Christ for worship, fellowship and communion with the Most High, in Jesus name.

- ....I rededicate the month to Christ for peace, prosperity and progress.(Breakthroughs, Healing, Fruitfulness, Promotion, Signs and Wonders, Victory....), in Jesus name.

- If I am at the gate of the month of .... with the wrong garment, Robe of Righteousness of Christ replace my garment, in Jesus name.

- Every hidden requirement of the gate of the month of ....(mention the name of the month) that must be fulfilled before I can prosper, but I know nothing about and cannot fulfill, sacrifice of Christ fulfill on my behalf,... on behalf of my spouse and children, in Jesus name.

- Laws of afflictions of month after month, I am no longer under law but under grace! D I E !!!! in Jesus name.

- Month of ...., hear the order from above, for my sake, disobey satanic laws assigned to frustrate me, in the name of Jesus.

- I replace the covenants that established the month but are anti-kingdom and anti-gospel, with the covenant of the blood of Jesus. O month of ....! yield no more to darkness for my sake, in Jesus name.

- Womb of the new month, bring forth with ease every essential ingredient of my breakthroughs and contradict every power of abortion of good things in the name of Jesus.

- What will identify me to my divine helper this month, but has been covered up by darkness, be made manifest by fire. In the name of Jesus.

- What will identify me to my divine helper this month, but has been covered up by household wickedness, be made manifest by fire, in the name of Jesus.

- As a sacrifice takes through the gate of the tabernacle, I tender the sacrifice of Christ to triumphantly take me through the gate of the month in the name of Jesus.

- O earth, O earth, O earth! It is written that you are my helper, reject anything buried in you to frustrate and waste me in the new month, in the name Jesus.

- Any blood shed to frustrate and waste my life in the new month, cry against your owner! in Jesus name.

- I replace the covenant that established the month (as __January____), with the covenant of the blood of Jesus and I rededicate the month to Christ for divine worship, Peace, Progress and Prosperity, in Jesus name.

- Month of .... as you are handing over to the month of ...., do so in my favor, in Jesus name.

- Month of ....as you are taking over from the month of ....do so in my favor and in the favor of my marriage, career and business, in Jesus name.

- As I am witnessing the beginning of the month so shall I witness the end in greater comfort and prosperity in the name of Jesus.

- The power of God that brought me through the closing month (year) successfully take me through the next month with greater success, in the name of Jesus.

- As last month ended on a note of joy, success, achievement, breakthrough, abundance, O new month begin on a better note! in the name Jesus.

- Regrets of last month perish with last month, and get not over into the new month in the name of Jesus.

- Ancestral spirits and family idols waiting at the gate of the month to renew evil covenants and dedications in my life, perish at the gate, in the name of Jesus.

- Family strongman waiting at the gate of the month to keep me out, die at the gate, in the name of Jesus.

- Sickness waiting at the gate of the month and seeking to gain entry with me, perish by the stripes of Christ, in Jesus name.

- The Spirit of God that in the beginning moved upon the waters and declared let there be light, I am at the beginning of the month, speak light into every darkness in my life, marriage, ministry, career and calling, in the name of Jesus.

- Mighty Jehovah, You are the initiator and terminator of time. Initiate my time of salvation and deliverance and terminate my time of bondage and hardship, in the name of Jesus.

- Mighty Jehovah, You are the initiator and terminator of time. Initiate my time of breakthrough and terminate my time of failure, in the name of Jesus.

- Mighty Jehovah, You are the initiator and terminator of time. Initiate my time of fruitfulness and multiplication and terminate my time of barrenness and unfruitfulness, in Jesus name.

- Satanic deadlines set up in the month looking at my age, hear the word of the Lord, by the spirit of Sarah, that does not pay attention to age in order to conceive, die !!!! in Jesus name.

- By the spirit of Sarah, that defied age and bore a son, I defy every satanic order contrary to my desired breakthroughs, in the name of Jesus.

- Any power using my age as a deadline to wear me out in the battles of life, die!!! in the name of Jesus.

- Any deadline of time set up in this month to put fear in me, die! in the name of Jesus.

- O Lord arise and terminate every Egyptian calendar operating in my life, in Jesus name.

- If my life is running on a satanic calendar, O Lord arise and change it now, in Jesus name.

- If my marriage is running on a satanic calendar, O Lord arise and change it now, in Jesus name.

- Register of tragedy and disaster of the new month, exclude my name and the name of every member of my household! in Jesus name.

- Evil consequences of the idolatrous transactions of the month's origin, exclude me and my household members in the name of Jesus.

Job38:22 Hast thou entered into the treasures of the snow? or hast thou seen the treasures of the hail, 23 Which I have reserved against the time of trouble, against the day of battle and war?

- If the month is a time of trouble, a time of battle and war, Jehovah, the Man of war fight for me and fight my battles, in the name of Jesus.

- If the day, week, month and year is a time of trouble, time of battle and war, Lord of Host, Jehovah Sabaoth, fight for me and fight my battles, in Jesus name .

- I release the month from every bondage of satanic dedications and covenants in the name of Jesus.

- Every demand for worship at the gate of the month that is not divine, perish by fire!, in the name of Jesus.

Power, Authority and Dominion in Christ

The preceding decrees, if taken without being a Priest and a King in Christ, will provoke serious attacks from the kingdom of darkness. You have no right to make those decrees. The gods you serve will come after you, treating you as an escapee! (Before coming to Christ every soul served the gods) And they would be right! You cannot leave the domain of the prince of this world, except Christ calls you out! To leave would tantamount to violations of standing orders. ***Isaiah 14:17 That made the world a wilderness, and destroyed the cities thereof, that opened not the prison to his prisoners?*** <u>Douay-Rheims Bible</u>

This is why some pray and are heavily attacked without any cover to shield them. The more they pray, the greater the attack! If you are none of Christ, you have no armor to "withstand the wiles of the devil". You are very prone to attacks of the enemy. This is your day of salvation! Quickly take the next decree 21 hot times !!!

- Lord Jesus the Christ, If I am none of yours, give me a repentant heart and a godly sorrow for my sins and make me one of yours. Accept me and cast me not out, in the name of Jesus.

- I take this moment as a moment of response to Christ's salvation call and I confess, renounce, repent and bring under the atoning cover of the blood of Jesus, my sins, the sins of my parents and of my ancestors that are standing against me to accuse me, in the name of Jesus.

- I take this moment as a moment of response to the call of Christ to salvation and I yield to Christ. I jump into Christ. Holy Spirit jump into me, in the name of Jesus.

- By the power of the call of Christ, I dissolve every evil spiritual marriage to powers promoting and sponsoring lust of the eyes, lust of the flesh and pride of life, in the name of Jesus.

- I subject my life, body, soul and spirit to the cleansing and atoning power of the blood of Jesus Christ, in the name of Jesus.

- Evil covenants in my blood assigned to keep me from coming to Christ, I am now in Christ, e x p i r e !!! in the name of Jesus.

- The life is in the blood. If my blood is such that cannot come to Christ and prosper, blood of Jesus replace my blood, molecule for molecule, atom for atom, in the name of Jesus.

- Dark altars of my father's house, place of birth and place of origin assigned to keep me from coming to Christ, I am now in Christ, collapse and die!!!, in the name of Jesus.

- I substitute my membership of the evil covenants of my father's house with my membership of the covenant of the blood of Jesus, in the name of Jesus.

CHAPTER 2

The Gregorian calendar

1 And the LORD spake unto Moses and Aaron in the land of Egypt, saying, 2 This month shall be unto you the beginning of months: it shall be the first month of the year to you. Exodus 12:1-2

Of the sons of Issachar, men who understood the times, with knowledge of what Israel should do,.....1 Chronicles 12:32

"So teach us to number our days that we may present to you a heart of wisdom" (Psalm 90:12)

The Calendar may look very harmless to the novice, but to the adept it is a very powerful tool and weapon that can be used to dominate, intimidate and manipulate. Every serious student of the school of advanced spiritual warfare, who is familiar with the concept of dedication, will always cautiously handle issues having to do with the calendar. What is a calendar?

A calendar is a system of organizing days for social, religious, commercial, or administrative purposes. This is done by giving names to periods of time, typically days, weeks, months, and years. The name given to each day is known as a date. Periods in a calendar (such as years and months) are usually, though not necessarily, synchronized with the cycle of the sun or the moon. Many civilizations and societies have devised a calendar, usually derived from other calendars on which they model their systems, suited to their particular needs.(Wikipedia)

Now this! If the cycle of the sun and the cycle of the moon are very vital in the set up of the calendar system, look at what powers have hijacked them as symbols and used them to create cult of worshipers. In the bible, the sun god is Baal and the Moon goddess is Semiramis, Queen of heaven, Ishtar, Asthoreth, Artemis, Diana.....

Ezekiel 8:16 "And he brought me into the inner

court of the Lord's house, and, behold, at the door of the temple of the Lord, between the porch and the altar, were about five and twenty men, with their backs toward the temple of the Lord, and their faces toward the east, and they worshiped the sun toward the east." Eze.viii,16.

Judges 2:13 And they forsook the LORD, and served Baal and Ashtaroth.

1Samuel 7:4 Then the children of Israel did put away Baalim and Ashtaroth, and served the LORD only.

Jeremiah 7:18 The children gather wood, and the fathers kindle the fire, and the women knead their dough, to make cakes to the queen of heaven, and to pour out drink offerings unto other gods, that they may provoke me to anger.

The set up of calendars that are based on the moon and the sun have strong imprints of the "sun-god" and "moon god".

The relationship between calendars and prayer might not be very clear from the first look. A calendar is what an average Christian has taken for granted in the most part simply because it looks too remote to affect daily life events. That the calendar has become a tool to afflict and oppress in the hand of the enemy is a fact unknown to many. Very few realize that the calendar has the power to kill just by virtue of what it has been created to do. The power of the calendar is the power of time and seasons. Syndromes of being at the right place at the wrong time are subjects of a lot of warfare prayers and decrees. "There is time for everything" the preacher declared in Ecclesiastes 3. A prayerful look at this important scripture will reveal the power of the calendar.

1 There is a time for everything,
and a season for every activity under heaven:
2 a time to be born and a time to die,
a time to plant and a time to uproot,
3 a time to kill and a time to heal,
a time to tear down and a time to build,
4 a time to weep and a time to laugh,
a time to mourn and a time to dance,
5 a time to scatter stones and a time to gather them,
a time to embrace and a time to refrain,
6 a time to search and a time to give up,
a time to keep and a time to throw away,
7 a time to tear and a time to mend,
a time to be silent and a time to speak,
8 a time to love and a time to hate,
a time for war and a time for peace.

It will amount to unnecessary struggle if you plant when it is time and season to uproot, if you are suing for peace when war is the only permissible language. The Sabbath, for example, is an element of time, therefore of the calendar. Accurate timing must be maintained in order not to violate it. The violation of the Sabbath was punishable by death. The power of the calendar is the subject of prayers in this book. The above referenced passage clearly shows the power of seasons and the danger of the doing the right thing at the wrong time. Or of doing the wrong thing at the right time. Or of being at the right place at the wrong time. Every one has run into statements like " if only you were here yesterday! You would have gotten the job." " if only he had crossed the bridge an hour before he would not have gone down with it" ...Those who passed through a bridge even one minute before it collapsed cannot but be ever grateful for time that was given in their favor. Who is controlling your time? Powers controlling your calendar are also controlling your time. My times are in your hands O Lord! the psalmist aggressively declared. Whatsoever has to do with the element of time, is an element of season, therefore an element of the calendar. Our God is often referred to as God of times and seasons. Paying attention to time is paying attention to the calendar. Who is in charge of the calendar of your life? Jesus or Julia?

Power of a Calendar and Prayer

The month is a period of the calendar, an element of time reckoning that is a subunit of the year. In the Gregorian calendar, it is derived from the time it takes the moon to go round the earth. Just as the year represent the time it takes the earth to go round the sun. Whose stamp is on this calendar and the periods (days, week, month and years) of the calendar? By what names are these periods called? Names are very important in spiritual warfare. "Naming is an exercise of sovereignty, proprietorship and role determination." Adam exercised this power of name and naming in the book of Genesis to the chagrin of Satan. The names of some were changed in scripture. Abram became Abraham. Sarai became Sarah. Jacob became Israel. Names are so important that the names of some in scripture were given before they were born. Ishmael, Isaac, Emmanuel, John. The names by which the month and days are referred to are very important spiritually.

We live in time, exist by time, prosper or fail in time and we die in time only to escape into eternity that is timeless. The date of birth and date of death are fixtures of time. The breakthroughs of life like all other events of life are at appointed time. "Is there not an appointed time to man upon earth?.....Job 7:1. However, the appointed time can be manipulated by the enemy. It can be made unavailable. You can run out of time and time can run out on you. Time can be wasted. The control of your time can reside in the hands of the enemy. No wonder the Psalmist shouted: "My times are in thy hand: deliver me from the hand of mine enemies, and from them that persecute me." Psalm 31:15. Like the psalmist, violently take this decree:

My times are in thy hand O Lord, I will not run out of time and my time will not run out for the good projects of my life, in the name of Jesus Christ.

If the control of my time is in the wrong hands, Holy Spirit take it out now and hold it forever, in the name of Jesus.

These transactions to which time can yield itself makes it highly imperative to pay careful attention to time and most importantly, regularly pray about time. Your time can become a powerful weapon that can be used against you by the enemy. This is one of the reasons why the prayers in this book will amount to a shock treatment to the enemy who had planned and hoped you will never come into knowledge of the secrets of time as laid out in this book. This is also the very reason why if you develop and cultivate the kingdom prayer culture of commanding time, particularly the month, dumbfounding and uncommon breakthroughs and testimonies will begin to appear in your life.

Have you ever felt like the number of hours in the day are not enough to accomplish the tasks of the day? Does it seem as if you are always running short of time? Are you always missing deadlines? Or always in battle with deadlines because you are one of those that procrastinate until you are close to the deadline? Are you a perpetual time-extension filer? Is the adversary of man in control of your time or your time is in the hands of the Almighty? Are there repeated problems in specific months of the year,

year after year? There are secrets of time you must acquire in order to terminate these afflictions.

"The ancient Hebrew poets, while meditating on the brevity of life, prayed, "So teach us to number our days that we may present to you a heart of wisdom" (Psalm 90:12). It was the inevitability of death that motivated this prayer for wisdom for living. This was a wisdom that didn't try to hide from the realities of life—be they joys or sorrows—but rather sought to keep finitude ever before it. Indeed the poem ends with a cry for God to "confirm the work of our hands." Numbering life's days led to meaningful engagement in work—and this was the mark of wisdom." (Slice of Infinity Series: Driven to Distraction by Margaret Manning)

"You must keep this ordinance at the appointed time year after year." Exodus 13:10 (NIV).

Missing the appointed time of the year to keep this ordinance would result in violation and of course with the attendant consequence.
This is a good ordinance given by the Most High for an appointed time, year after year. By the same token, a satanic ordinance can be issued for a particular month, year after year. I am familiar with a sister who always lose her job in a particular month of the year. She has resigned to her fate, according to her. She only prepares herself once the month is approaching. This of course means she cannot keep a job for more than twelve months. Strange and

mysterious problems! These are the type of problems that send people deliverance-seeking. What satanic ordinances have been inscribed on the cycle of the moon or the sun for your sake? Shout:

Thou power of repeated problems assigned to frustrate me in life, die!!! in the name of Jesus.

Every affliction of year after year originating from a curse, expire!!! in the name of Jesus.

Can Time Be Commanded? Can the Month be commanded? Students of advanced spiritual warfare have learned the secrets of commanding the day by commanding the morning. The ending of the preceding year, month, week and day should and must end up in the operation of laying the foundation for the next year, month, week and day. The approaching cycle, the incoming cycle has to be commanded….. Hast thou commanded the day….Job declared. He could have equally declared, hast thou commanded the week, the month or the year? All these could not however remain "un-commanded". Either you do it or someone else would do it for you.

Job 38:12 Hast thou commanded the morning since thy days; and caused the dayspring to know his place;
13 That it might take hold of the ends of the earth, that the wicked might be shaken out of it?

The morning is an element of time and it can be commanded. Every period of time, day, week, month and year can be commanded. Joshua spoke to the sun that rules the day and the moon that rules the night and they obeyed him.

Joshua 10:12 Then spake Joshua to the LORD in the day when the LORD delivered up the Amorites before the children of Israel, and he said in the sight of Israel, Sun, stand thou still upon Gibeon; and thou, Moon, in the valley of Ajalon.
13 And the sun stood still, and the moon stayed, until the people had avenged themselves upon their enemies. Is not this written in the book of Jasher? So the sun stood still in the midst of heaven, and hasted not to go down about a whole day.
14 And there was no day like that before it or after it, that the LORD hearkened unto the voice of a man: for the LORD fought for Israel.

Joshua commanded time and it stood still till the enemies were utterly destroyed. The element of time obeyed the instructions of Joshua. There is an anointing of Joshua that commands and gets results. Shout:

As Joshua commanded the sun and the moon and they obeyed, I command the month to accommodate my breakthroughs in the name of Jesus.

Commanding a cycle should be done in conformity

with the attributes and characteristics of the cycle. The way and manner the day of Sabbath is commanded will never be the way the 2nd or 3rd day of the week would be commanded? You would not command the day of Sabbath for any other purpose than the purpose of the kingdom, of worship, of service, of sacrifice and of praise.

- *Mighty Jehovah, You are the initiator and terminator of time. Initiate my time of salvation and deliverance and terminate my time of bondage and hardship, in the name of Jesus.*

- *Mighty Jehovah, You are the initiator and terminator of time. Initiate my time of breakthrough and terminate my time of failure, in the name of Jesus.*

- *Mighty Jehovah, You are the initiator and terminator of time. Initiate my time of fruitfulness and multiplication and terminate my time of barrenness and unfruitfulness, in the name of Jesus.*

- *Stars of heaven, as you fought against Sisera, fight for me against my stubborn pursuers, in the name of Jesus.*

CHAPTER 3

Who can command the month?

Priests and Kings in Christ are the only ones who are qualified to command like Joshua. Inappropriately issued commands can provoke a "sons of Sceva effect". (Acts 19:13-16.) And the situation can get worse instead of getting better. You lack a relationship with Christ and you cannot command the month. As a matter of fact, you can command nothing and the days are evil.

The days are evil........

"To use time wisely "because the days are evil" is a curious phrase embedded in the inspired language of the Apostle Paul in Ephesians 5:15-16: "Therefore be careful how you walk, not as unwise men, but as wise, making the most of your time, because the days are evil" (NASB). Paul may have exhorted the Christians at Ephesus to make the most of their time because he and/or the Ephesians were experiencing persecution or opposition (such as in Acts 19:23-20:1). In any event, we need to use every moment with wisdom "because the days are evil" still."

"Even without the kind of persecution or opposition known by the Christians of Paul's days, the world we live in is not conducive to using time wisely, especially for purposes of spirituality and Godliness. In fact, our days are days of active evil. There are great thieves of time that are minions of the world, the flesh, and the Devil. They may range in form from high-tech, socially acceptable preoccupations to simple, idle talk or ungoverned thoughts. *But the natural course of our minds, our bodies, our world, and our days leads us toward evil, not toward Christlikeness*." (DW)

Why command the Month?

I enjoin every reader that has come this far, to please take every decree that comes along in the course of this book very seriously. Each of the decrees, I mean every one of the decrees has a suite of breakthroughs in marriage, career, ministry and life in general, attached. These are practical prayers for practical and instantaneous result as you subject the powers behind your troubles to a shock treatment in so far they do not expect you to know of their existence, not to mention praying against them. The prayers, as strange as they may sound, are Holy-Ghost-engineered for specific results.

Many run out of time for the good projects of life and they have their time run out for endeavors that would have made them great. Forcefully decree!

My time will not run out and I will not run out of time for the good projects that would get me fulfilled in the name of Jesus.

Why do you need to command the month? Can the month be commanded? Who can command the month? To whom would the month yield in command? How do you command the month?

Many Christians have not come to realize the importance of praying about time and praying on time. They keep wondering why at the end of every day they feel like they have accomplished nothing. Feeling unaccomplished at the end of the day frustrates many and creates stress that is making many to age quickly. There are secrets to time and the usage of time. There are spiritual transactions that governs and rule the secrets of time and the Most High has given us cues in his word if only we would listen!

Our objective is to command the month at the right time and lay the foundation of the month on a solid rock that would support our breakthroughs and progress of the month in the month. A quick look at power of dedicated time in scripture will open your eyes as to why the enemy seeks to capture your time in order to hold you captive.

Concept of Gates of entry into every month

What is a gate? A gate is an accessing point in time and space. A gate is a place of control. A place of traffic. A place of transition. A place of deliberation and meeting. A place of summon. The beginning of every month serve as a gate into the month. The beginning of the day, week, month and year serves as a gate of entry. A very important lessons about gates can be culled from the gate of the tabernacle. Every gate has requirements of entry. The gate of every country has visa requirements. The gate of the tabernacle has requirements and can only be accessed with appropriate sacrifice. By the same token, as every month is unique, the gate of each month, the threshold of each month is unique by virtue of ordinal position and by virtue of the dedications made of each month.

As a sacrifice takes you through the gate of the tabernacle, i tender the sacrifice of Christ to take me through the gate of the month, in Jesus name.

O gate of the month become my gate of prosperity, healing and breakthroughs in the name of Jesus.

The gate can be controlled. Whoever controls the gate controls the traffic through the gate. The gate can be manipulated. The gate can be programmed for good and for evil. There are secrets to gates. The gate can serve as a spiritual entity. "Lift up your heads, O Ye gates!" If the gate can lift up its head, the gate can respond to orders appropriately given.

The gates of my father's house that have predetermined how far I can go in life, I no longer subscribe to you. I subscribe to the gate that is Christ. Lose your power over my life, in the name of Jesus

The gates of my place of origin that are remote-controlling the kind of breakthroughs the indigenes can receive, count me out, I am now in Christ, in the name of Jesus.

Idolatrous background of the Calendar and months.

The days are evil and time has become a highly dedicated commodity."Whoever created paganism has been running the world for a long time. Everyday the entire world wakes up to a pagan day of the week. The Greeks named the days of the week after the sun, the moon and the five known planets….Mars, Mercury, Jupiter, Venus and Saturn, which in turn are named after the Greek gods, Ares, Hermes, Zeus, Aphrodite and Cronus. The Greeks called the days of the week the Theon Hemerai which means "days of the gods". The romans substituted their equivalent gods for the greek gods. Mars, Mercury, Jove (Jupiter), Venus and Saturn. The Germanic peoples substituted similar gods for the Roman gods. Tiu (twia), Wooden, Thor, Freya (Fria) but did not substitute Saturn."

The present western calendar was instituted by Pope Gregory hence the name Gregorian. It is based on the Julian calendar that has been in place since the roman empire. However, do not be fooled. The origin of the months, particularly as indicated by the names of the months, has the signature of the ruler of this world, Satan, on it. And therein lies a great evil. Time has become a highly dedicated commodity that is now made available at will of the enemy. The days of the week are dedicated. The months are dedicated. Even in some eastern calendars, the years are dedicated. What does it mean to have time dedicated?

Power of Dedication

The Concept of Dedication

The loss of power, authority and dominion in the garden of Eden, resulted also in the loss of control over one of the most important element of life, TIME! Many are running a rat race because of the perpetual battle with time. Many are losing in the battles of life simply because they run out of time in the execution of projects that would have led to fulfillment of their destiny. Many have become casualties in the battles of life, because they ran out of time. Shoot!

- ***Every battle for my time, be always decided in my favor in the name of Jesus Christ.***

Of the sons of Issachar, men who understood the times, with knowledge of what Israel should do,.....1 Chronicles 12:32.

Men of Issachar have this singular and unique qualification that sets them apart in scripture. This highly loaded verse of scripture holds the key that is missing in the lives of many who have failed in life. Understanding the times and knowing what ought to be done at any given time is a recipe for good success. The sons of Issachar have been divinely credited to have this capability of understanding the times and knowing what ought to be done by Israel. Whenever this kind of statement could be made about you, be very sure you have joined the exclusive club of the champions! Are many not lost today simply because they do not know who they are and what they are supposed to be doing? The generation of baby boomers and generation X are like a ship that has lost its rudder in the high and mighty seas of life. What is it about time, about that crucial gate called time that has always eluded man and it's still eluding him?

Evil dedications of time assigned to rob me of time, die! in the name of Jesus.

The answer to the question lies in a proper understanding of the concept of dedication. The dedication of time and space.

What is Dedication ?

: an act or rite of <u>dedicating</u> to a divine being or to a sacred use

: a devoting or setting aside for a particular purpose

To dedicate means to set apart for a deity or for religious purposes; to consecrate; to set apart for special use.

In this definition lies the key of the secret why man will always run into a battle for time and with time. To have something dedicated is to render such unavailable for any other purpose other than that to which it has been dedicated. Something dedicated can only be successfully used for the purpose of the dedication. A vehicle dedicated to space travel will not find an easy use for travel on land without adequate changes being made. You can only dedicate what you own. Dedication smirks of ownership. I need to own a building before I can dedicate it for use as a public library. Every other usage must expressly come with my permission, which I am free to grant or deny. God Himself started out with the dedication of the time of the seventh day to rest.

Genesis 2:1 Thus the heavens and the earth were finished, and all the host of them.

2 And on the seventh day God ended His work which He had done; and He rested on the seventh day from all His work which He had done.(A)

3 And God blessed (spoke good of) the seventh day, set it apart as His own, and hallowed it, because on it God rested from all His work which He had

created and done.

The Lord set the seventh day apart. He sanctified the seventh day. You cannot use the time of the seventh day for your whims and caprices without consequence. It must be used for what He has prescribed. Listen to the book of Exodus on this.

Exodus 20:11 For in six days the LORD made the heavens and the earth, the sea, and all that is in them, but he rested on the seventh day. Therefore the LORD blessed the Sabbath day and made it holy.

Exodus 31:17 It will be a sign between me and the Israelites forever, for in six days the LORD made the heavens and the earth, and on the seventh day he abstained from work and rested.'"

Now look at the consequence of flouting this covenant!

Exodus 31:15 For six days, work is to be done, but the seventh day is a Sabbath of rest, holy to the LORD. Whoever does any work on the Sabbath day must be put to death. 16The Israelites are to observe the Sabbath, celebrating it for the generations to come as a lasting covenant.

Dedicated time cannot be used for something else without consequence. The enemy always seek to mimic God and by this token has moved to have days of the week, months and years dedicated to himself in order to further his agenda to steal, kill and destroy. The enemy is using the power of evil dedication to make time unavailable to man to fulfill his divine destiny. The control exerted over time by the enemy serves very well his evil agenda. Man has been placed in a position to always feel the need to pursue time and to no avail.

Isa 58:13 If thou turn away thy foot from the Sabbath, from doing thy pleasure on my holy day; and call the Sabbath a delight, the holy of the LORD, honorable; and shalt honor him, not doing thine own ways, nor finding thine own pleasure, nor speaking thine own words: Isa 58:14 Then shalt thou delight thyself in the LORD; and I will cause thee to ride upon the high places of the earth, and feed thee with the heritage of Jacob thy father: for the mouth of the LORD hath spoken it.

There are blessings and favor bestowed for obedience to purpose of dedication just as there is repercussion for disobedience of purpose of dedication.

Are there things you cannot do on a dedicated day? See what Jesus was expected not to do on Sabbath?

Matthew 12:10

(10) And behold, there was a man who had a withered hand. And they asked Him, saying, "Is it lawful to heal on the Sabbath?"—that they might accuse Him.

Mark 3:1-2

(1) And He entered the synagogue again, and a man was there who had a withered hand. (2) So they watched Him closely, whether He would heal him on the Sabbath, so that they might accuse Him.

Luke 6:7

(7) So the scribes and Pharisees watched Him closely, whether He would heal on the Sabbath, that they might find an accusation against Him.

Though theirs was a misconstrue, they had knowledge that certain things can be done and some not, on dedicated days.

If the month has been satanically programmed to be unavailable for my breakthroughs, I take the power of Christ and I de-program it, in the name of Jesus

Upon the loss of power, authority and dominion in the garden of Eden, the enemy not only took over the control of man, he also took over the control of the time of man. Henceforth time would become a need of man, with control of the need in the hands of Satan. The need of man for time suddenly became a tool in the hands of Satan to manipulate man. It would be used by Satan to coerce man into giving worship to beggarly gods in furtherance of the satanic agenda. Your conscious or unconscious worship of the gods would pollute you. A polluted man can never enjoy divine presence. Outside of divine presence there is nothing but gloomy darkness. The joy-forevermore is only possible in the presence of the divine. Worship something else and you can never worship true God except when salvaged by Christ. If man would always need time for every activity under the sun, and the time is only available when granted by beggarly gods who will only grant time in exchange for worship? thereby polluting man and keep man out of divine presence, where he belongs, time has become the bane of the man without Christ. And those with Christ but are ignorant suffer the same fate.

The Most High took one day, the seventh day and set it apart for rest and himself. The gods took the seven and captured the month and years thereby. Every day of the week is dedicated to gods who have hijacked the heavenly objects that have captured the attention of man, as their symbols and have the days dedicated to such heavenly bodies.

The core of the decrees taken to command the month would be decrees that undo evil dedications thereby requiring knowledge of the origin of the Gregorian calendar and the constituent months.

Thrones and stools are responsible for the formulation of calendars. Thrones and stools are altars and they are dedicated to the gods of this world. Only altars expressly dedicated to Jehovah are excluded. Since the Cross of Christ, the issue of altars has been settled. The death of Christ was a sacrifice for our redemption. The Lamb, Passover lamb of God that takes away the sins of the world, was offered in sacrifice for our sins. Every sacrifice requires an altar. The altar of sacrifice of Christ, the Sacrifice and the resultant blood covenant are Ultimate that have the trio issues of altars, sacrifice and covenant settled for ever. The Most High has been satisfied by these trio of altar, sacrifice and covenant of Christ and He is no more interested in any other. Every altar, sacrifice and covenant of today that is not subscribing to the Ultimate of Christ are anti-Christ and will incur the wrath of God.

The names of the days of the week have a pagan origin just like the months. The Most High took one day, the seventh day and set it apart for rest and himself. The gods took the seven and captured the month and years thereby. Every day of the week is dedicated to gods who have hijacked the heavenly objects that have captured the attention of man, as their symbols and have the days dedicated to such heavenly symbols personifying these evil spirits. Sunday for Sun. Monday for Moon.....etc

The Naming of the Days

Sunday -- Sun's day

Monday -- Moon's day

Tuesday -- Tiu's day

Wednesday -- Woden's day

Thursday -- Thor's day

Friday -- Freya's day

Saturday -- Saturn's day

The Greeks named the days of the week after the sun, the moon and the five known planets, which were in turn named after the gods Ares, Hermes, Zeus, Aphrodite, and Cronus. The sun-god is referred to as Baal in scriptures. The Greeks called the days of the week the Theon hemerai "days of the Gods". The Romans substituted their equivalent gods for the Greek gods, Mars, Mercury, Jove (Jupiter), Venus, and Saturn. (The two pantheons are very similar.) The Germanic peoples generally substituted roughly similar gods for the Roman gods, Tiu (Twia), Woden, Thor, Freya (Fria), but did not substitute Saturn.

"In the history of mankind no form of idolatry has been more widely practiced than that of the worship of the sun. It may well be described as universal; for there is scarcely a nation in which the worship of the sun in some form has not found a place. In Egypt, the oldest nation of historic times, under the names of Ra and Osiris, with half a dozen other forms; in Phenicia and the land of Canaan, under the names of Baal, Melkarth, Shamas, Adoni, Moloch, and many other forms; in Syria, Tammuz and Elagabalus; among the Moabites, under the names of Baal-peor and Chemosh; among the Babylonians and Assyrians, under the names of Bel and Shamas; among the Medes and Persians and other kindred nations, under the name of Ormuz and Mithra; among the ancient Indians, under the name of Mitra, Mithra, or Mithras;1 in Greece, under Adonis, Apollo, Bacchus, and Hercules; in Phrygia, under the term Atys; and in Rome, under Bacchus, Apollo, and Hercules; -- in all these places, and under all these forms, the sun was worshiped by all these peoples. The myth of Hercules alone will illustrate the wide-spread practice of this worship: "The mythology of Hercules is of a very mixed character in the form in which it has come down to us. There is in it the identification of one or more Grecian heroes with Melcarth, the sun-god of the Phenicians. hence we find Hercules so frequently represented as the sun-god, and his twelve labors regarded as the passage of the sun through the twelve signs of the zodiac. he is the powerful planet which animates and imparts fecundity to the universe, whose divinity has been honored in every quarter by temples and altars, and consecrated in the religious strains of all national. From Meroe in Ethiopia, and Thebes in Upper Egypt, even to Britain, and the icy regions of Scythia; from the ancient Taprobana and Palibothra in India, to Cadiz and the shores of the Atlantic; from the forests of Germany to the burning sands of Africa; -- everywhere, in short, where the benefits of the luminary of day are experienced, there we find established the name and worship of a Hercules." (Ancient Sun Worship and Its Impact on Christianity. By A.T Jones)

Theon Hemerai, the greeks commonly say. The days of the gods. The gods of the nations also via the planets rule the days of the week by having the days dedicated to themselves. Yes, dedicated! Dedication smirks of ownership. They feign owning time too. The gods of the nations. They named the months to suit their whims and caprices. The ninth to the twelfth month are all bearing names contrary to their numerical and ordinal positions in the calendar. The ninth month is called the seventh (Sept) by name, the tenth month is called the eighth (Octo), the eleventh month is called the ninth (Novem), the twelvth is called the tenth (Decima) and no wonder these last four months are notorious for tragedies and disasters of a closing quota.

The Lord is interested in the calendar of man. He changed the calendar of Israel as they left Egypt.

The Lord said to Moses and Aaron in the land of Egypt, 2 "This month shall be for you the beginning of months. It shall be the first month of the year for you. Exodus 12:1-2

To have left the calendar unchanged would have meant that the affairs of the children of Israel would proceed according to the Egyptian calendar.

- **If my life has been following a satanic calendar, I disengage it now, in the name of**

Jesus.

- O Lord arise and terminate every Egyptian calendar operating in my life, in the name of Jesus.

- If my life is running on a satanic calendar, O Lord arise and change it now, in the name of Jesus.

- If my marriage is running on a satanic calendar, O Lord change it now, in the name of Jesus.

- The covenants that established this day as Sunday by dedicating the day to the sun-god, be replaced by the covenant of the blood of Jesus and break!, in the name of Jesus.

- The covenants that established this day as Monday by having the day dedicated to the moon god, break by the covenant of the blood of Jesus, in the name of Jesus.

- The covenants that established this day as Tuesday by having the day dedicated to the

god of war, Tiu, break by the covenant of the blood of Jesus.

The calendar is always a product of agreement, a covenant. People who make use of the calendar consciously or unconsciously become members of the covenant. Who inspired the covenant? God or Satan?

Every month of the western world calendar has spiritual characteristics pointing to a definitely idolatrous background and origin. This is not without consequence when it comes to the battle for the control of time. Some spiritual powers are struggling to be in control of your time. They pretend they have the time dedicated to themselves and can only release it for the use of man in exchange for worship. Command the Month gives you the spiritual tools to take back the control and administration of time that the adversary has arrogated to himself.

Practical prayer that speaks to the idolatrous root of the Julian and Gregorian calendar system is what this book is all about.

Some hidden and thriving serpents and scorpions are about to be uncovered in your life as you read this book. Do not be ignorant of his devices. The only antidote to ignorance is acquisition of knowledge. True knowledge of the true God first and foremost but also knowledge of the adversary so that you would not be ignorant of his devices. There is knowledge about time you need to acquire to undo the strategy of the enemy on time. This strategy has the sole purpose of stealing, killing and destroying destinies.

Every month has a womb of good things and of bad things that are made available to those who know how to reach for them.

There are keys of prayers that can unlock the womb of the month and render the content available. The keys are unique as the months are unique. There are secrets of success of every month that can only be made available to the spiritually discerning.

There are accomplishments that would continue to elude many in a month until they come into the secrets of success of that month. Every month has riches, wealth and prosperity locked into them that can only be made available to the spiritually discerning in Christ.

Those who are yoked to Christ and specifically demand for the secrets of the month are the ones who will have it. The truth is, very few fall into this category. Why ? Many do not even know they are missing out on something. Many do not know they are in the midst of a declared war ! A war that originated in heaven . " Rev.12:7 And there was war in heaven." Many do not know they have an enemy by the name "Hinderer". The greatest success of this enemy is to make people believe he does not exist. Only an identified enemy can be conquered. An elusive enemy is very difficult to overcome.

if there is anything the enemy has secretly taken control of in the bid to successfully steal, kill and destroy, it is time. If your time has been captured, you have been captured. No wonder the psalmist cried out " my times are in your hand" Psalm 31:15.

Things can be made to happen before the appointed time. Read this!

Matthew 8:29 And behold, they cried out, "What have you to do with us, O Son of God? Have you come here to torment us before the time?"

The ordinal and numerical position of each of the twelve months of the year bear spiritual significance in spiritual warfare. Time is so uniquely precious that it would be unthinkable that the avowed enemy of the soul of man would leave it untouched and untainted by his schemes to steal, kill and destroy. Capture the time of man and you would have captured man himself. The enemy, right from the exit of man from the garden of Eden, seeks to capture time by having time dedicated to himself. The enemy of course watched the dedication of the 7th day to God and took a cue to mimic God.

CHAPTER 4

A History of the Months and the Meanings of their Names

January -- Janus's month
February -- month of Februa
Intercalaris -- inter-calendar month
March -- Mars' month
April -- Aphrodite's month
May -- Maia's month
June -- Juno's month
July -- Julius Caesar's month
August -- Augustus Caesar's month
September -- the seventh month
October -- the eighth month
November -- the ninth month
December -- the tenth month

A History of the Months

The original Roman year had 10 named months Martius "March", Aprilis "April", Maius "May", Junius "June", Quintilis "July", Sextilis "August", September "September", October "October", November "November", December "December", and probably two unnamed months in the dead of winter when not much happened in agriculture. The year began with Martius "March". Numa Pompilius, the second king of Rome circa 700 BC, added the two months Januarius "January" and Februarius "February". He also moved the beginning of the year from Marius to Januarius and changed the number of days in several months to be odd, a lucky number. After Februarius there was occasionally an additional month of Intercalaris "intercalendar". This is the origin of the leap-year day being in February. In 46 BC, Julius Caesar reformed the Roman calendar (hence the Julian calendar) changing the number of days in many months and removing Intercalaris.

The calendar of the western world of today is a product of idolatrous Roman Empire. Calendar is a product of agreement, thus a covenant. Agreement is the basis of any Calendar. The users passively or actively agree to the reckoning of time for all time-related transactions. Spiritually, the calendar assumes an extraordinary significance seeing that the Lord chose to change the calendar of Israel as they were about to leave Egypt, the land of bondage, where they had lived for 430 years.

Exodus 12:1 The Lord said to Moses and Aaron in the land of Egypt, 2 "This month shall be for you the beginning of months. It shall be the first month of the year for you.

This is the institution of the Hebrew calendar. Their lives have been patterned before this on an Egyptian calendar. The calendar of the oppressors. Of course the Egyptian calendar was dedicated to the gods of Egypt. Continued subscription to that calendar would mean subscribing to the gods of the land of Egypt. We may not be able to change our calendar in the physical but we can pray against the consequences of idolatrous calendar. We have the dominion in Christ to address issues that seems "landlocked" and irreversible. While we may not be able to change the calendar, we can nullify the evil effects thereof. We can ask the consequences thereof to exclude us and our household members. We can asks the dedications that came into place when we subscribe to the gods behind the calendars to expire and break! We can dissociate ourselves from the covenants supporting the calendar.

Biblical transactions reflecting the numerical position of the month in the calendar system are borrowed out of scriptures to qualify our months and pray accordingly. The first month has qualities of 1, the second month the qualities of 2 and so on. These qualities and peculiarities can be invoked. Command the month makes use of these biblical transactions and characteristics.

- *I dissociate myself from all evil covenants that I know nothing about but are supporting the calendar I employ for time reckoning, in the name of Jesus.*

- *Thou power of idolatrous calendar upon my life, die, in the name of Jesus.*

- *Unconscious evil dedication of the months to the gods through the Gregorian calendar, take the sacrifice of Christ and break, in the name of Jesus.*

- *Consequences of idolatrous calendar upon my destiny, be thou removed by the blood of Jesus Christ.*

- *If my life is following the dictates of the gods of idolatrous calendar, O God arise and deliver me, in the name of Jesus.*

- *Evil covenants woven and smuggled into idolatrous calendars affecting my destiny, be revoked, overruled and replaced by the covenant of the blood of Jesus, in the name of Jesus.*

- *Where is the God that changed the calendar of Israel in the land of Egypt, change every calendar negatively affecting my life, marriage, career and business, in the name of Jesus.*

- *Kingdom calendar replace every idolatrous calendar affecting my life, in the name of Jesus.*

- *Witchcraft calendars assigned to frustrate me in life, marriage and career, I set you ablaze!*

- *Calendars not in my favor, die! in the name of Jesus.*

CHAPTER 5

Command the First Month: January.

Ex12:2 This month is to be your beginning of months; it will be your first month of the year.

Exodus 40:1 And the LORD spake unto Moses, saying, 2 On the first day of the first month shalt thou set up the tabernacle of the tent of the congregation.

January is the first month of the year in the Julian and Gregorian calendars and one of seven months with the length of 31 days. The first day of the month is known as New Year's Day. It is, on average, the coldest month of the year within most of the Northern Hemisphere (where it is the second month of winter) and the warmest month of the year within most of the Southern Hemisphere (where it is the second month of summer). In the Southern hemisphere, January is the seasonal equivalent of July in the Northern hemisphere.

January is named after Janus (Ianuarius) and therefore dedicated to Janus, the god of the doorway; the name has its beginnings in Roman mythology, coming from the Latin word for door (ianua) – January is the door to the year. Traditionally, the original Roman calendar consisted of 10 months, totalling 304 days, winter being considered a monthless period. Around 713 BC, the semi-mythical successor of Romulus, King Numa Pompilius, is supposed to have added the months of January and February, allowing the calendar to equal a standard lunar year (365 days). Although March was originally the first month in the old Roman Calendar, January became the first month of the calendar year under either Numa or the Decemvirs about 450 BC (Roman writers differ). In contrast, specific years pertaining to dates were identified by naming two consuls, who entered office on May 1 and March 15 until 153 BC, when they began to enter office on January 1.

I tender the sacrifice of Christ to undo every evil dedication of the first month January to Janus and I rededicate the month to Christ for divine worship, divine favor and divine provision....for breakthrough, healing, deliverance and promotion, in the name of Jesus.

The decree you have just taken shows the need to command the month against powers of evil dedication. This is fundamental and highly required for the command of the month. Evil dedication as explained in earlier chapters renders the month unavailable for your progress and prosperity.

The numeral 1 is a unique number. It is a number that represent the Divine and the unity of the Divine. "There can be no doubt as to the significance of this primary number. In all languages it is the symbol of unity. As a cardinal number it denotes unity; as an ordinal it denotes primacy. Unity being indivisible, and not made up of other numbers, is therefore independent of all others, and is the source of all others. So with the Deity. The great First Cause is independent of all. All stand in need of Him, and He needs no assistance from any." (E.W. Bullinger Numbers in Scripture")

The first month occupies a truly unique position. The first day of the month marks also the first day of the year. This gate of time is highly significant in the warfare for time. The transactions of this primal gate captures the successive bigger periods of time. Month, seasons, years, decades or even millennium. At these gates of the day, month and year you undertake warfare transactions with grave consequence for the whole year. This is why the enemy values these gates as places in time continuum, where havocs are wreaked on the uninformed.

The foundation laying of the month is also the foundation laying of the new year. It is a cross over transaction. A beginning transaction. As a matter of great importance in scriptures, the Passover transaction became a transaction of the beginning of the months. A salvational transaction. A deliverance transaction. The Passover transaction is a January-like transaction!

Ex12:2   This month is to be your beginning of months; it will be your first month of the year.

What makes the month of Passover become the first month of Jewish calendar? The month of deliverance from the bondage of Egypt by divine decree becomes the first month for a reason. It speaks the mind of God as to what the first month should be and look like. If we had doubts in our mind as to what the first month should reflect, God Himself has shown it in his decree. Total freedom to worship the Divine in truth and in spirit is available for those knowledgeable in Christ enough to ask for it.

Starting up the year, the first month must carry divine attention. The purpose and plan of God must be made clear for the month and for the year. Divine worship, fellowship, obedience, consecration, sanctification are issues that must characterize the first month. The tabernacle set-up is a first month transaction. Your worship of the Divine occupies a position of foundational importance. God first. "Seek ye first the kingdom of God and His righteousness; and all these things shall be added unto you." Matt.6:33

Ex 40;17 So the tabernacle was set up on the first

day of the first month, in the second year.

Gen.1:1 In the beginning, God created the heavens and the earth. 2 The earth was without form and void, and darkness was over the face of the deep. And the Spirit of God was hovering over the face of the waters.

- *As the first month is unique, my breakthroughs be unique. in the name of Jesus.*

- **The Spirit of God that moved upon the waters in the beginning and declared let there be light, i am at the beginning of the year and the month, speak light into every darkness in my life, marriage, ministry, career and calling, in the name of Jesus.**

- **As the first month marks the beginning of the year, O month of January, mark the beginning of better things in my life, marriage, career and business in the name of Jesus.**

- **As January is first among months, among equals, competitors and peers I shall be first, in Jesus name.**

- **Power of the first in the month of January, incubate me for promotion, in the name of Jesus.**

- **The gods honored by January, I will not honor you. I honor only Christ!!!**

- **The covenants that established January be replaced for my sake and the sake of everything that pertains to me by the covenant of the blood of Jesus, in the mighty name of Jesus.**

- **As the first month, January, cannot be demoted, I will not be demoted, in the name of Jesus.**

- **As January cannot but come first, I cannot but come first among my equals and competitors, in the name of Jesus.**

- **As January marks the Passover from the old to new, I pass over from failure in life to success in life, in the name of Jesus.**

- **As January marks the crossover from the old year to the new year, I cross over from profitless transactions of the old year to profitable transactions of the new year in the name of Jesus.**

- **Where is the God that promoted the month**

Nisan to be the first month for the Israelites in Egypt, promote me to be the first among my equals and competitors this month and this year, in the name of Jesus.

Ezekiel 30:20 In the eleventh year, in the first month ...., the word of the LORD came to me:

The Lord sent His word to Ezekiel in the first month, O Lord, this is the first month, send me your word that will prosper me, ...promote me....change my story for the best, ...lift up my head above my contemporaries,...heal me from every sickness in my body, soul and spirit, in the mighty name of Jesus

Ezra 7:9 For upon the first day of the first month began he to go up from Babylon; and on the first day of the fifth month came he to Jerusalem, according to the good hand of his God upon him.
- **In the first month Ezra began to go up from Babylon of captivity. This is the first month and I go out of every captivity assigned to waste my life**
- **.... every captivity assigned to keep me lonely**
- **....every captivity of prolonged singleness**

Genesis 8:13 By the first day of the first month of Noah's six hundred and first year, the water had dried up from the earth. Noah then removed the covering from the ark and saw that the surface of the ground was dry.

- **In the first month Noah witnessed the floodwater dry up. This is the first month, flood of affliction in my life, dry up!**

- **The power of God that dried up the flood water in the first month, this is the first month show up again and dry up every flood of affliction, of shame and disgrace in my life.**

2 Chronicles 29:3 In the first month of the first year of his reign, he opened the doors of the temple of the LORD and repaired them.

- **The doors of the temple of the Lord were opened in the first month. I am the temple of the Holy Spirit, O Lord, open the door of my heart to your words, this is the first month.**

Numbers 33;3 The Israelites set out from Rameses on the fifteenth day of the first month, the day after the Passover. They marched out boldly in full view of all the Egyptians,

- **In the first month, Israel marched out boldly out of Egypt in full view of all Egyptians. I march out boldly out of every bondage of darkness in full view of all my stubborn pursuers.**

Joel 2:23 Be glad then, you children of Zion, and rejoice in the LORD your God: for he has given you the former rain moderately, and he will cause to come down for you the rain, the former rain, and the latter rain in the first month.

- **By reason of the first month, I claim the rain, the former rain and the latter rain of blessing in every area of my life, in the name of Jesus.**

- **If my blood is subscribing to covenants I know nothing about, I unsubscribe by the power in the blood of Jesus.**

- **Whosoever has been engaged by Satan to speak negative words into the atmosphere about me and my life, refuse to do the job, in the name of Jesus.**

- **Days of January, you will not become dates of sorrow and tragedy, in the name of Jesus.**

- **Every deadline of time in January, assigned to wear me out like a garment, perish in the name of Jesus.**

CHAPTER 6

Command the second month: February

Genesis 7:1 In the six hundredth year of Noah's life, in the second month, on the seventeenth day of the month, on that day all the fountains of the great deep burst forth, and the windows of the heavens were opened.

Genesis 8:4 In the second month, ..., the earth had dried out.

February is the second month of the year in the Julian and Gregorian calendars. It is the shortest month and the only month with fewer than 30 days. The month has 29 days in leap years, when the year number is divisible by four (except for years that are divisible by 100 and not by 400 in the Gregorian calendar). In common years the month has 28 days.

February starts on the same day of the week as March and November in common years, and on the same day of the week as August in leap years. February ends on the same day of the week as October every year and January in common years only.

February was named after the Latin term februum, which means purification, via the purification ritual Februa held on February 15 in the old Roman calendar. January and February were the last two months to be added to the Roman calendar, since the Romans originally considered winter a monthless period. They were added by Numa Pompilius about 700 BC. February remained the last month of the calendar year until the time of the decemvirs (c. 450 BC), when it became the second month.

February is dedicated to purification festival. The Lord cleansed the earth with a flood in the second month. Cleansing, purification and sanctifications are transactions that could be easily invoked in the second month. The month of February will yield itself to cleansing from addictions, habits and vices.

By Genesis 7:1 I initiate the cleansing required of my life, body, soul and spirit by the power of the blood of Jesus.

- **The idolatrous covenants that established February, be replaced by the covenant of the blood of Jesus, in the mighty name of Jesus**

- **The covenants that gave birth to February will not give birth to failure, tragedy and disaster in my life, in the name of Jesus**

Significance of two

The power of second is the power of difference considering that the unity of one does not permit a difference.

February exercises the rights of the second to be different. February has the singular and unique quality to be the only month among the twelve of the year to be with 28/29 days. Very unique qualities can be called and spoken into being in the second month. The unique flood of Noah, for God promised never to destroy the earth again with water, commenced in the second month. But the earth also dried out in the second month.

Genesis 7:1 In the six hundredth year of Noah's life, in the second month, on the seventeenth day of the month, on that day all the fountains of the great deep burst forth, and the windows of the heavens were opened.

- *In the second month you flooded the earth to cleanse it. Flood my life with the blood of Jesus for cleansing, purification and sanctification, in the name of Jesus*

- *Powers assigned against the glory of my star in February, look at Christ and die, in* the name of Jesus

- *Observer of time assigned against my life in February, die!, in the name of Jesus*

- *Evil dedication of the day, week and month that is not allowing me a profitable use of the time of the day, week and month, die in the name of Jesus.*

- *Holy Spirit undo every evil dedication of the day, week and month programmed to rob me of a profitable use of my time.*

- *If the time of this day, week and month is not available to me for prosperity, progress, breakthrough, peace, peace in marriage, happiness in marriage, fulfillment in marriage, marital breakthrough, success because of evil dedication, My Father break the dedication! in the name of Jesus.*

....Blood of Jesus break the dedication
....Lord Jesus break the dedication
....fire of God break the dedication!!! In the name of Jesus.

- *If, because of evil dedication, the time of this day, week, and month is not available that my helpers may locate me, Holy Spirit break the dedication in the name of Jesus.*

- *If the time of this day, week, and month is*

not available to me to seek first the kingdom of God and it's righteousness, Holy Spirit make it available in Jesus name.

CHAPTER 7

Command the Third Month: March

Esther 8:9 The king's scribes were summoned at that time, in the third month, which is the month of Sivan, ...

March is the third month of the year in the Gregorian Calendar, and one of the seven months which are 31 days long.
March in the Southern Hemisphere is the seasonal equivalent of September in the Northern Hemisphere. In the Northern hemisphere, the beginning of the meteorological spring is 1 March. In the Southern hemisphere, the beginning of the meteorological autumn is 1 March.
The name of March comes from ancient Rome, when March was the first month of the year and named Martius after Mars, the Roman god of war. In Rome,

where the climate is Mediterranean, March was the first month of spring, a logical point for the beginning of the year as well as the start of the military campaign season. January became the first month of the calendar year either under King Numa Pompilius (c. 713 BC) or under the Decemvirs about 450 BC (Roman writers differ).

Activities of war are prominently enabled by the enemy in the third month. It is the customary season of war. Dedication of the month to Roman god of war gives clear evidence of transactions and activities favored in the third month. War is always accompanied by bloodshed. The gods of the nations who require bloodshed in sacrificial worship look forward to the third month to have it. Fighting spirits and the ministry of conflict always go hand in hand in the third month.

Spiritual Significance of Three

Three is the first of four perfect numbers.
Three denotes divine perfection;
Seven denotes spiritual perfection;
Ten denotes ordinal perfection; and
Twelve denotes governmental perfection.
Hence the number three points us to what is real, essential, perfect, substantial, complete, and Divine. There is nothing real in man or of man. Everything "under the sun" and apart from God is "vanity." "Every man at his best estate is altogether vanity" (Psa 139:5,11, 62:9, 144:4; Eccl 1:2,4, 2:11,17,26, 3:19, 4:4, 11:8, 12:8; Rom 8:20).

Three is the number associated with the Godhead, for there are "three persons in one God." Three times the Seraphim cry, "Holy, Holy, Holy"--one for each of the three persons in the Trinity (Isa 6:3). The living creatures also in Revelation 4:8.

Three times is the blessing given in Numbers 6:23, 24:--

"The LORD bless thee and keep thee (the Father);

The LORD make His face shine upon thee; and be gracious unto thee (the Son)

The LORD lift up His countenance upon thee, and give thee peace" (the Holy Spirit).

- Powers that dedicated the third month to war, I am dedicated to the prince of peace, count me and my household out of your evil dedication in the name of Jesus.

- Powers demanding for blood in the month of war, become drunken with your own blood as with sweet wine, in the name of Jesus.

- Tragedies and disasters associated with war, my life is not available, exclude me and my household, in the name of Jesus.

- Blood-thirsty demons of the third month, the life is in the blood! drink your own blood like sweet wine, my blood has become the blood of Jesus and cannot be drunken!, in the name of Jesus

- The spirit of the enemy that is being given to

people to fuel war, will not be given to me or members of my household, in the name of Jesus.

- The spirit of the enemy that promotes war in the third month die and never prosper in my life, in the name of Jesus.

- Coven activities programmed for the third month, to promote strife in my life, scatter, in the name of Jesus.

- Month of March! Do not cooperate with my enemies, in the name of Jesus.

- Holy Spirit inspire and determine my thoughts and actions of the third month, the month of March, in the name of Jesus

- Holy Spirit inspire, determine and establish my steps as I go through this month and year, in the name of Jesus

Genesis1: 9 And God said, "Let the water under the sky be gathered to one place, and let dry ground appear." And it was so. 10 God called the dry ground "land," and the gathered waters he called "seas." And God saw that it was good.
11Then God said, "Let the land produce vegetation: seed-bearing plants and trees on the land that bear fruit with seed in it, according to their various kinds." And it was so. 12The land produced vegetation:

plants bearing seed according to their kinds and trees bearing fruit with seed in it according to their kinds. And God saw that it was good. 13And there was evening, and there was morning—the third day.

- As the third day of creation witnessed the separation of the water from the land, let the third month witness the permanent separation of affliction from my life, marriage and ministry, in the name of Jesus.

- Power of God that separated water from land on the third day, this is the third month, separate my life from the bondages and collective captivity of my father's house, mother's house, place of birth and place of origin, in the name of Jesus.

CHAPTER 8

Command the Fourth Month: April

2Samuel 11:1 In the spring of the year, when kings normally go out to war, David sent Joab and the Israelite army to fight the Ammonites. They destroyed the Ammonite army and laid siege to the city of Rabbah. However, David stayed behind in Jerusalem.(NLT)

Genesis 1:14 And God said, "Let there be lights in the expanse of the heavens to separate the day from the night. And let them be for signs and for seasons, [6] and for days and years, 15 and let them be lights in the expanse of the heavens to give light upon the earth." And it was so. 16 And God made the two great lights—the greater light to rule the day and the lesser light to rule the night—and the stars.

17 And God set them in the expanse of the heavens to give light on the earth, 18 to rule over the day and over the night, and to separate the light from the darkness. And God saw that it was good. 19 And there was evening and there was morning, the fourth day.

Ezekiel 1:1 In the thirtieth year, in the fourth month, on the fifth day of the month, as I was among the exiles by the Chebar canal, the heavens were opened, and I saw visions of God.

Of course the third and the fourth months are in the same period. War and war and war!. Hear what a researcher has to say!

"Is there something about this time of year that lends itself to madness? Winter is fading and spring is beginning to show itself. Some people believe that long winters can cause a type of madness. Is there any truth to this? Could it be the extra push these lunatics needed to commit these horrible tragedies? I find it very bizarre that this week is the anniversary of so many horrific tragedies. I find it worrisome that this month (April) carries so many tragedies. I have to wonder what else I would find if I were to dig deeper. What do you think?" (Chaotic Ramblings)

Spiritual Significance of Four
Now the number four is made up of three and one (3+1=4), and it denotes, therefore, and marks that

which follows the revelation of God in the Trinity, namely, His creative works. He is known by the things that are seen. Hence the written revelation commences with the words, "In-the-beginning God CREATED." Creation is therefore the next thing—the fourth thing, and the number four always has reference to all that is created. It is emphatically the number of Creation. (E.W Bullinger)

April is the fourth month of the year in the Gregorian Calendar, and one of four months with a length of 30 days. April was originally the second month of the Roman calendar, before January and February were added by King Numa Pompilius about 700 BC. It became the fourth month of the calendar year (the year when twelve months are displayed in order) during the time of the decemvirs about 450 BC, when it also was given 29 days. The derivation of the name (Latin Aprilis) is uncertain. The traditional etymology is from the Latin aperire, "to open," in allusion to its being the season when trees and flowers begin to "open," which is supported by comparison with the modern Greek use of άνοιξις (opening) for spring. Since some of the Roman months were named in honor of divinities, and as April was sacred to Venus, the Festum Veneris et Fortunae Virilis being held on the first day, it has been suggested that Aprilis was originally her month Aphrilis, from her Greek name Aphrodite (Aphros), or from the Etruscan name Apru. Jacob Grimm suggests the name of a hypothetical god or hero, Aper or Aprus.[1]

The Anglo-Saxons called April Oster-monath or

Eostur-monath. The Venerable Bede says that this month is the root of the word Easter. He further speculates that the month was named after a goddess Eostre whose feast was in that month. St George's day is the twenty-third of the month; and St Mark's Eve, with its superstition that the ghosts of those who are doomed to die within the year will be seen to pass into the church, falls on the twenty-fourth. In China the symbolic ploughing of the earth by the emperor and princes of the blood takes place in their third month, which frequently corresponds to our April. The Finns called (and still call) this month Huhtikuu, or 'Burnwood Month', when the wood for beat and burn clearing of farmland was felled.

The dedication of the fourth month to Venus or Aphrodite as the god is known in greek is an indication of the type of manipulation, affliction and bondage the month would accommodate.
Transactions of conflict and strife are rife in the fourth Month by name April.

"April has to be one of the bloodiest months of the year. After watching the news and doing research, I've come to realize that many massacres and terrible events have occurred during the bloody month of April over the years. ...."
"A breakdown of the most recent atrocities committed during this bizarrely, tragic week of the bloody month of April follows.

April 19, 1993 - Waco Tragedy
The 51-day Branch Davidian standoff, with the

Bureau of Alcohol, Tobacco, Fire Arms and Explosives, in Waco, Texas ends in the fiery death of approximately 76 people, including 27 children.
For more information on this date in history, visit April 19

April 19, 1995 - Oklahoma City Bombing
The deadly bombing of the Alfred P. Murrah Federal Building, a government building in Oklahoma City, Oklahoma took place killing 168 people and injuring over 800 more.
For more information on this date in history, visit April 19

April 20, 1999 - Columbine School Shooting
Two deranged students stalk classmates and teachers killing twelve students and one teacher before killing themselves at the Columbine High School in Colorado.
For more information on this date in history, visit April 20

April 16, 2007 - VA Tech Massacre
Crazed lunatic kills two students in the early hours of the morning and then goes across the campus of VA Tech to kill 30 more students and wound nearly 30 more.
For more information on this date in history, visit April 16

The Bloody Month of April
Wars that began during the month of April are:
The American Revolution (1775)

The American Civil War (1861)
The Armenian Genocide (1914)
The Bosnian War (1992)
The Rwandan Genocide (1994)"

Blood must be shed in April but it will not be your blood! The life is in the blood. The offering of blood is the offering of life. Venus is of course Semiramis. The queen of heaven! With seat in the moon. The Anglo-Saxons call April "Oster-Monath" . The month of Oster. From where we have the word Easter. This is the same as the biblical Astarte or Ashtaroth. Violence, war and bloodshed are the trade marks of queen of heaven. And April is dedicated to this deity. That explains the bloodshed of Spring. It is not a coincidence that April of Spring is dedicated to the queen of heaven. This goddess is bloodthirsty! She is responsible for major tragedies and disasters like earthquakes, plane crash, accidents, religious clashes, tribal wars and everything that spills blood!

- *I tender the sacrifice of Christ to undo every evil dedication of the fourth month to war and gods and goddesses of war, in the name of Jesus.*

- *Blood-drinking altars of April, dedicated to the queen of heaven, my blood is not available, die! in the name of Jesus.*

- *Bloodshed agenda of the queen of heaven in the fourth month, exclude me and my household members, in the name of Jesus.*

- *O moon ! you shall not smite me by night! in the name of Jesus.*

- *You heavens! do not cooperate with bloodshed agenda of the fourth month assigned against me, in the name of Jesus.*

- *I release my destiny from the grip of evil sacrifice offered to the queen of heaven in the fourth month, in the mighty name of Jesus.*

....I release my marriage.....
....I release my career.....
....I release my business....

- *The queen of heaven of my place of birth, release my glory by fire, in the name of Jesus.*

- *Every influence of the queen of heaven over my finances in the fourth month die! in Jesus name.*

- *By the spirit of Ezekiel that experienced open heavens and divine visions in the fourth month, my heavens in the month of April, my heavens of the fourth month open by fire, in Jesus name.*

- *Open heavens of the fourth month locate*

me now, this is the fourth month, in Jesus name.

- *The power using my giving to devour me, my giving must enrich me, fall down and die, in the name of Jesus.*

- *Whosoever I am giving to but he's taking all that I have, lose your demonic power now, in the name of Jesus.*

- *Whosoever I have given to and has demonically taken all that I have, give back what i did not give you, in the name of Jesus.*

- *Progress arresters of my father's house and mother's house assigned against me in the fourth month, be arrested and die, in the name Jesus.*

- *Activities of coffin spirits, power of coffin spirits assigned against us in the month of April, die! in the name of Jesus.*

- *Activities of coffin spirits assigned against my good projects of the month of April, die! in Jesus name.*

- *Market places of darkness trading in the virtues that would make me great, scatter and die! in the name of Jesus.*

- *O God arise and destroy the mask of my "frenemies", enemies posing as friend, in the name of Jesus.*

- *Anointing of empty-handedness in the house of God, you are anointing of poverty, my life is not available to you, die! in Jesus name.*

- *As Christ did not spend one day longer than necessary in the wilderness, I will not spend one day longer than necessary in this stubborn situation of unemployment ....this joblessness, loneliness, disappointment, etc!, in the name of Jesus.*

- *Prosperity divinely attached to my destiny but now in the grip of house-hold wickedness, hear the order from above, come out now and come out quick, in the name of Jesus.*

CHAPTER 9

Command the Fifth Month: May The Month of Grace

Ezra 7:8-9 And he came to Jerusalem in the fifth month, which was in the seventh year of the king. 9 For upon the first day of the first month began he to go up from Babylon, and on the first day of the fifth month came he to Jerusalem, according to the good hand of his God upon him
Ezra 7:8-9 (KJV)

20 And God said, Let the waters bring forth abundantly the moving creature that hath life, and fowl that may fly above the earth in the open firmament of heaven. 21 And God created great whales, and every living creature that moveth, which

the waters brought forth abundantly, after their kind, and every winged fowl after his kind: and God saw that it was good. 22 And God blessed them, saying, Be fruitful, and multiply, and fill the waters in the seas, and let fowl multiply in the earth. 23 And the evening and the morning were the fifth day.
Gen 1:20-23 (KJV)

May is the fifth month of the year in the Julian and Gregorian Calendars and one of seven months with the length of 31 days.

The month May was named for the Greek goddess Maia, who was identified with the Roman era goddess of fertility, Bona Dea, whose festival was held in May. Conversely, the Roman poet Ovid provides a second etymology, in which he says that the month of May is named for the maiores, Latin for "elders," and that the following month (June) is named for the iuniores, or "young people" (Fasti VI.88).
In both common Western calendrical systems, no other month begins on the same day of the week as May. The months of May and June are the only two which have this trait.

SPIRITUAL SIGNIFICANCE OF FIVE

"Five is four plus one (4+1). We have had hitherto the three persons of the Godhead, and their manifestation in creation. Now we have a further revelation of a People called out from mankind, redeemed and saved, to walk with God from earth to heaven. Hence, Redemption follows creation.

Inasmuch as in consequence of the fall of man creation came under the curse and was "made subject to vanity," therefore man and creation must be redeemed. Thus we have:

Father
Son
Spirit
Creation
Redemption

These are the five great mysteries, and five is therefore the number of GRACE.
If four is the number of the world, then it represents man's weakness, and helplessness, and vanity, as we have seen.
But four plus one (4+1=5) is significant of Divine strength added to and made perfect in that weakness; of omnipotence combined with the impotence of earth; of Divine favour uninfluenced and invincible." (E.W Bullinger)

- My door of greatness of the fifth month, open now by the power in the blood of Jesus.

- O month of May, you will not disappear with my breakthroughs and blessings.

- 2 peter1:4. By the promises of God, I am a participant of divine nature and I escape the corruption in the world caused by evil desires, in the name of Jesus.

- By the promises of God I will suffer no demotion, bewitchment, rejection, disappointment or sickness in the fifth month, in the name of Jesus.

- By violent faith I provoke the manifestation of my breakthroughs of the month of grace, in the name of Jesus.

- Holy Spirit do your works in my life to increase my brokenness, in the name of Jesus.

- Properties of darkness in my life and body catch fire! in Jesus name.

- None given to Christ was lost, no one given to be saved through the word of God in my mouth shall be lost nor remain unsaved!, in the name of Jesus.

- Padlocks of marine witchcraft that have locked up the joy of my marriage, break and die! in the name of Jesus.

- Padlocks of marine witchcraft that has locked up the fruitfulness in my marriage, break and die, in the name of Jesus.

- Strange taste and strange appetite assigned to pollute and waste my life, die! in the name of Jesus.

- Strange taste and strange appetite inherited from my parents, die, in the name of Jesus.

- Strange taste and strange appetite from my father's house, place of birth and place of origin, die, in the name of Jesus.

- I blow back whatsoever was blown on me in the dream, in the name of Jesus.

- The gods that have taken the time of the fifth month by evil dedication, give it back to Christ and give it back to me, in the name of Jesus.

- Power of evil dedication handing over my time of the fifth month to the gods of my father's house, of my place of birth and place of origin die and leave my time alone, in the name of Jesus.

- Gen.1:20-23 The fruitfulness and multiplication of the fifth day of creation, this is the fifth month of grace, manifest in my life
- ....manifest and swallow every lack, poverty and barrenness in my life, marriage and career, in the name of Jesus.

- Fruitfulness and multiplication of the fifth day of creation, translate into my fruitfulness and multiplication in this fifth month of grace, in the name of Jesus.

- Spiritual blindness inherited from my father's house and will not allow me to see good things, die, in Jesus name.

- Spiritual blindness inherited from my place of birth and origin and has negatively conditioned my vision, die, in the name of Jesus.

- In the name of Jesus Christ, Apostle Paul commanded the spirit of divination (spirit of python) to leave the slave girl and it left. In the name of Jesus Christ I command every spirit in and around me that is contrary to spirit of God to leave and never return, in the name of Jesus. (Acts 16:18)

- Every spirit responsible for lack and poverty in my life, die, in the name of Jesus.

- Every spirit that will not allow me to improve myself and do more for God Jehovah, die, in Jesus name.

- Every Spirit blocking miracles in my life, die, in the mighty name of Jesus Christ.

- The slave girl was delivered from the spirit of python. I lay claim to total, complete and permanent deliverance from the spirit of divination, in the name of Jesus.

- Lord Jesus, You called Lazarus out of the

grave, call me out of darkness.

- Lord Jesus, you called Lazarus out of the grip of death, call me out of the grip of marine witchcraft, lack and poverty, disappointment.....

- Wicked powers that have re-packaged my life for the archive of "almost there", archive of worthless history, die, in the name Jesus.

- If my story is a story of sitting for the wrong examination, O God arise and change my story, in Jesus name.

- If my story is a story of winning the race God did not ask me to run, O God arise and change my story, in the name of Jesus.

- Tragedy programmed for my eyes to witness, scatter, in the name of Jesus.

- Thou word of God, by your virtue as a Hammer, break the evil chains tying me down in barrenness, failure, and poverty in the name of Jesus.

- Thou word of God, by your virtue as fire, consume every evil chain on my hands and feet arresting my labor and progress.

- Holy Spirit give me the power to excel for you and to excel in your service, in the name of Jesus.

- Thou word of God, by your virtue as hammer, break down every opposition to my progress in life, in Jesus name.

- Thou word of God by your virtue as fire and hammer search the land of the living and the dead and waste my wasters, in Jesus name.

- Holy Spirit do your work in me that I may excel for you and excel in your service, in Jesus name.

- What I should have gotten 25years ago (long time ago) and is now manifesting, appear with every blessing, opportunity and breakthrough that I have missed, in the name of Jesus Christ..

- I cast down every evil imagination projected to pollute and keep me polluted, in Jesus name.

- Evil covenant between my father's house and the streams of my place of origin work in vain! in Jesus name.

- Evil dedications of my father's house, place of birth and place of origin, demanding for renewal by sacrifice, take the sacrifice of Christ and lose your hold upon my life, in the name of Jesus.

- Altars of my father's house, pursuing me for a

sacrifice I cannot give, collide with Rock of Ages and perish, in the name of Jesus.

- Sacrificial demands of the evil altars of my father's house and place of origin take the sacrifice of Christ and expire! in the name of Jesus.

- Curses issued out of retaliation and out of anger, by whosoever felt offended by me, Christ has redeemed me from the curse of the law, break! in the name of Jesus.

- The curses my anger has provoked in the past and are still operating in my life, break now by the blood of Christ!, in the name of Jesus.

- Curses that will not allow me to hold on to good things, break! in the name of Jesus.

- I demand the physical manifestation of the qualities and virtues that made me the winner on my night of conception, in the name of Jesus.

- The qualities that made me (mention your name) a winner on my night of conception, but the wickedness (household wickedness) of my father's house has hijacked, be released now for immediate manifestation, in the name of Jesus.

- Every damage I suffered while my virtues were

missing, be repaired by the blood of Jesus, in the name of Jesus.

- Any power that is envious of my glory and wants to use my glory to shine, die without my glory! in the name of Jesus.

- Argumentative spirit deposited in my life by my father's house, my place of birth and my place of origin to waste my life, die! in the name of Jesus.

- Every attack of "you shall see" that has become the root of my stubborn situation, backfire and die! in Jesus name.

- Whosoever is angry with me but pretending not to be, be exposed and let the evil thoughts in your heart perish, in Jesus name.

- Every enemy pretending to be a friend in order to waste me, be exposed! in the name of Jesus.

- Every hand ever laid on my head and has caused me damage, I take away your damage by the blood of Jesus, in Jesus name.

- Every damage my glory has suffered because of every contrary hand ever laid on my head, be undone by the blood of Jesus.

- Dark dedications of my father's house making me to rise and fall, die without renewal and die without success, in the name of Jesus.

- The power in my mother that is acting like my mother to arrest my progress, be arrested and die, in Jesus name.

- "Get and lose" spirit from my father's house, leave me alone and die, in Jesus name.

- Family yokes making me to get and lose, break, in Jesus name.

- Family curse of get and lose, break by the blood of Jesus, in Jesus name.

- The curse on my father's house, making me to get and lose, break by the blood of Jesus.

- .....that is not allowing me to hold on to good things, in the name of Jesus.

- Seconds, minutes and hours of my life, deliver good things into my life, in Jesus name

- The arrows of death which I escaped in the past shall not rise again, for it is written, afflictions shall not rise again the second time, in Jesus name

- Elements of nature, forces of nature, shall not yield to the voice of death for my sake and for the sake of my wife, in the name of Jesus.

- Blood-thirsty altars of my father's house, I shall not become your victim, in Jesus.

- Blood-thirsty altars of my father's house, I will not become your victim on my day of glory, in Jesus name.

- Pronouncement of envious souls upon my life, career and marriage, die, in Jesus name.

- The curses issued by whosoever I offended unknowingly in the past, Christ has redeemed me from the curse of the law, break, in Jesus name.

- Curses issued by my step-mothers break by the blood of Jesus!

- My situation become a testimony that Jehovah God is my God, in the name of Jesus.

- My life become a testimony that I have encountered Christ and the Holy Spirit is in me, in Jesus name.

- The days of the week that are not available to me for progress and prosperity because they have been dedicated to gods that are not Christ, become available by the power of Christ, in the name of Jesus.

- Favor of God drink sorrow out of my life, in the name of Jesus.

- Every pollution I have suffered from anger, pride, lust and un-forgiveness, I tender the sacrifice of Christ as payment and I employ the blood of Christ to remove it, in Jesus name.

- Progress-arresting pollution of the dream and of the night, die, in the name of Jesus.

- Barrenness-imposing pollution of the night and of the dream, be removed by the blood of Jesus, in Jesus name.

- Poverty activators of the dream and of the night, die, in Jesus name.

- Contrary powers of my present location, die, in Jesus name.

- Contrary powers of my place of employment, die, in Jesus name.

- Contrary powers of my place of marriage, die, in Jesus name.

- Anything stolen from my life when I was a baby and it's keeping me from greatness, arise and locate me, in Jesus name.

- If the money I am giving out to help others has

become my devourer, Holy Spirit kill the devourer in the name of Jesus Christ.

- Chronicles 4:10 Jabez alludes to his name, "sorrowful": "Grant O Lord. that the grief implied in my name may not come upon me, in the name of Jesus!"

- Doctrine of salvation by self-efforts, you are a doctrine of untruth, die with every spirit attached to you and die from the root, in Jesus name.

- Spirits using disorder, lies, hatred, lust, un-forgiveness, pride, anger to prosper in my life, die, in Jesus name.

- Evil spirits attached to sexual immorality, disorder, lies, lust, anger, pride, un-forgiveness, in my life, die with your attachments in Jesus name.

- Powers using anger to pollute me and keep me polluted, be destroyed in the name of Jesus.

- Every dedication of any day of the week to the spirit spouse be undone in the name of Jesus.

- Any power, any spirit wife/husband taking the days of the week as their dedicated properties, leave the days alone and die! in the name of Jesus.

Acts 17:16 Now while Paul was waiting for them at Athens, his spirit was provoked within him as he saw that the city was full of idols.

- As the spirit of Paul was provoked within him for a city full of idols, my spirit be provoked against the idols of my heart! in the name of Jesus.

- Whatsoever is making what belongs to me to be easily taken away from me, die, in the name of Jesus.

- Curse of "Get it and lose it" operating in my life, break by the blood of Jesus.

- The damage to my life and foundation that is not allowing my life and foundation to carry my desired breakthrough be undone by the power of Christ, in the name of Jesus.

- Grace for greater obedience and greater brokenness fall and rest upon me, in the name of Jesus.

- O God arise and repair my foundation to carry uncommon breakthroughs, in the name of Jesus.

- Any power rearranging my steps to a place where I cannot be blessed, die! In the name of Jesus.

- If my name has positioned me for failure in life, Holy Spirit change my name in the spirit and in the physical, in the name of Jesus.

- Whatever is making the angel of blessing to avoid me, die! in Jesus name.

- if my father's house will not let me go out and prosper like Abraham, Voice of Christ call me out. (Genesis 12:1)

- Whatsoever extra luggage I have in my hands and its excluding prosperity from my life, I drop it by force, in the name of Jesus.

- If my foundation is not allowing me to go and prosper, kingdom of God replace my foundation, in the name of Jesus.

- If my foundation is faulty, I send it to the workshop of the Lord for repairs now, now, now! in Jesus name.

- If my foundation is not fitted for prosperity, Holy Spirit visit my foundation and refit it for breakthroughs, in Jesus name.

- If I am doing the business of God in a manner inappropriate, I enter into divine grace, for repentance and godly sorrow for my sins, in Jesus name.

- If I am using a dull axe to cut the tree of sin in my life, I exchange it for a divine axe, in the name of Jesus.

- If the conveyor of my life is not appropriate for my desired breakthrough, I exchange it with the conveyor of the Lord.

- If the evil powers of my father's house will not allow me to be married and remain happily married, I summon them for permanent destruction in the name of Jesus.

- If the vehicle of my life has broken down and I have been bewitched not to know it, Divine workshop call it up for repair for the sake of Christ, in the name Jesus.

- If I am wrongly positioned for the breakthroughs of the fifth month,
  Holy Spirit reposition me, in the name of Jesus.

Judges 7:4 But the LORD told Gideon, "There are still too many! Bring them down to the spring, and I will test them to determine who will go with you and who will not."

- Holy spirit test those that will be coming to me today and reveal those you have not ordained to come to me, in the name of Jesus.

- My inner man! Why are you sleeping? Wake

up! in the name of Jesus.

- If access to my personal mysteries has been blocked, mercy of God unblock it now, in the name of Jesus.

- If I am doing things heaven has ordained I should not do, mercy of God in Christ, stop it now. (Samson was ordained not to marry Delilah, and he did and was "de-glorified")

- if I have done what heaven has forbidden me to do, mercy of God in Christ, undo my deeds, in the name of Jesus.

- Holy Spirit show me myself and decode my life/my situation, in the name of Jesus.

- Any power asking me to sit on the floor when I have been given a comfortable seat, sit on the floor and die on the floor, in the name of Jesus.

- Wicked powers, demoting powers (of my father's house) asking me to sit on the floor when heaven has provided me a throne, sit on the floor and die on the floor, in the name of Jesus.

- Power instigating those around me and things around me to become monitors of darkness, die, in the name of Jesus.

- Powers turning things and those around me

into monitors of darkness die! in the name of Jesus.

- Evil pronouncements and curses that have tied me down where I do not belong, break! in the name of Jesus.

- I have been ordained to go and be fruitful, every power punishing me for doing so, die, in the name of Jesus.

- Anything that does not correspond to the purpose and will of God for my life, die! in the name of Jesus.

- Any power that is not Yahweh and calling me spouse, you are a liar, die, in the name of Jesus.

- Yahshuah HaMaschiach, make me one of yours and keep me one of yours.

- Hell-bound souls of my place of residence come now in the net of the gospel of Christ! in the name of Jesus.

- The Powers of my father's house supervising the program of evil monitor in my life and in my environment, die, in the name of Jesus.

- Evil Programs of my father's house constituting souls and things around me into evil monitors of darkness, crash and scatter ! in the name of

Jesus.

CHAPTER 10

Command the Sixth Month: June

26 And in the sixth month the angel Gabriel was sent from God unto a city of Galilee, named Nazareth, 27 To a virgin espoused to a man whose name was Joseph, of the house of David; and the virgin's name was Mary.
Luke 1:26-27 (KJV)

June is the sixth month of the year in the Julian and Gregorian calendars and one of the four months with a length of 30 days. Ovid provides two etymologies for June's name in his poem concerning the months entitled the Fasti. The first is that the month is named after the Roman goddess Juno, wife of Jupiter and equivalent to the Greek goddess Hera, whilst the second is that the name comes from the Latin word iuniores, meaning "younger ones," as opposed to maiores ("elders") for which the preceding month May is named.

Juno is the principle goddess of the Roman Pantheon. She is the goddess of marriage and the well-being of women. She is the wife and sister of Jupiter. She is identified with the Greek goddess Hera.

Juno is another name for the queen of heaven. The sixth month is dedicated to the queen of heaven.

"Queen of Heaven with the ancient Phoenicians, was Astarte; Greeks, Hera; Romans, Juno; Trivia, Hecate, Diana, the Egyptian Isis, etc., were all so called; but with the Roman Catholics it is the Virgin Mary."

Children conceived in the sixth month are due to arrive the next year spring. A time of war. Chemosh, god of the Moabites and Molech, god of the Ammonites are worshipped by burning of babies, offered by their own parents. " In worshipping any god, you must sacrifice something that the god gives. To worship the god of fertility the people had temple prostitution and offered child sacrifices." (False gods of biblical times: Nelson Illustrated Bible Dictionary, Theological Wordbook of the Old Testament, christiangays.com)

To understand this practice just described look at this scripture: Genesis 19:30-38
Lot and His Daughters
30Lot and his two daughters left Zoar and settled in

the mountains, for he was afraid to stay in Zoar. He and his two daughters lived in a cave. 31One day the older daughter said to the younger, "Our father is old, and there is no man around here to lie with us, as is the custom all over the earth. 32Let's get our father to drink wine and then lie with him and preserve our family line through our father."

33That night they got their father to drink wine, and the older daughter went in and lay with him. He was not aware of it when she lay down or when she got up.

34The next day the older daughter said to the younger, "Last night I lay with my father. Let's get him to drink wine again tonight, and you go in and lie with him so we can preserve our family line through our father." 35So they got their father to drink wine that night also, and the younger daughter went and lay with him. Again he was not aware of it when she lay down or when she got up.

36So both of Lot's daughters became pregnant by their father. 37The older daughter had a son, and she named him Moab; he is the father of the Moabites of today. 38The younger daughter also had a son, and she named him Ben-Ammi; he is the father of the Ammonites of today. (NIV)

The transactions described in this scripture showed the origin of the national gods of the Moabites and Ammonites. Chemosh and Molech or Moloch. The daughters of Lot offered their fertility! The gods that are worshipped by virginity and fertility surely inspired their decision to sleep with their father. The Queen of heaven, Juno, is conversant and familiar with warped relationships, being wife and sister of Jupiter at the same time. The two daughters of Lot became mother and sister of their sons at the same time; They have the same father. It is not too far-fetched to cite their source of inspiration as Semiramis, Queen of heaven, Diana, Artemis.............

If your month of conception happened to be in June, and that is probably the case if you were born anywhere in Spring months of March-April, then take this prayer:

- **This is my month of conception. Every transaction of my conception that is contrary to my divine destiny, be reversed and undone by the power of Christ, in the name of Jesus.**

- **Moab and Ben-Ammi were conceived under influence of alcohol. Every ungodly and unholy transaction that influenced my conception, lose your grip upon my glory, I am now in Christ, in the name of Jesus.**

- **The daughters of Lot used alcohol to manipulate the conception of their children. Everything ungodly employed by my parents to manipulate my conception, stop affecting my glory! in the name of Jesus. (destiny, life, marital life, marriage, children, taste, appetite, desires, progress, prosperity.....), in the name of Jesus.**

- **My Father, deliver me from the strange taste and habit originating from the transactions of my conception, in the name of Jesus.**

- **Sexual misconduct of the daughters of Lot made their sons enemies of God. Sexual misconducts of my parents making me an enemy of God, lose your power! in the name of Jesus.**

- **Power of the sexual misconducts of my parents and ancestors to manipulate my destiny and glory, die! in the name of Jesus.**

- **I reject strange and ungodly source of inspiration. Holy Spirit ! be my only source of inspiration, in the name of Jesus.**

SPIRITUAL SIGNIFICANCE OF SIX

Six is either 4 plus 2, i.e., man's world (4) with man's enmity to God (2) brought in: or it is 5 plus 1, the grace of God made of none effect by man's addition to it, or perversion, or corruption of it: or it is 7 minus 1, i.e., man's coming short of spiritual perfection. In any case, therefore, it has to do with man; it is the number of imperfection; the human number; the number of MAN as destitute of God, without God, without Christ.

At any rate it is certain that man was created on the sixth day, and thus he has the number six impressed upon him. Moreover, six days were appointed to him for his labour; while one day is associated in sovereignty with the Lord God, as His rest.

Six, therefore, is the number of labour also, of man's labour as apart and distinct from God's rest. True, it marks the completion of Creation as God's work, and therefore the number is significant of secular completeness.

The serpent also was created on the sixth day.

- **I approach the throne of grace with the sacrifice of Christ as a sacrifice of thanksgiving for divine access to breakthroughs of the sixth month, in the name of Jesus.**

- **Evil covenants made with the month of July for my sake, the sake of my marriage/marital life, break, in the name of Jesus.**

- **Transactions of favor of the sixth month bombard my life and career in the name of Jesus.**

- **Transactions of good news of the sixth month bombard my life, in the name of Jesus.**

- **Miracle of the virgin birth was initiated in the sixth month. Miracles that will change my story, appear now, this is sixth month. (Luke1)**

- Miracle of the virgin birth was initiated in the sixth month. Miracles that will usher me into my next level in life, ministry and career appear now in the name of Jesus.

- The power of God that overshadowed Mary for a miracle in the sixth month, overshadow me for a miracle, in the name of Jesus.

- The favor of God that located Mary and swallowed her fear, locate me and swallow my fear, doubts, discouragement, anxieties and weakness, in the name of Jesus.

- On the sixth day, man, the cream of creation, was made. Power to successfully and prosperously create in the sixth month locate me, in the name of Jesus.

- Power of creativity and innovation of the sixth day of creation, incubate me, this is the sixth month, in the name of Jesus.

- The sixth month favored angelic transaction. O month of June, favor angelic transactions in my life, marriage, career and ministry, in the name of Jesus.

- Every evil spiritual marriage that has witnessed the beginning of today, you will not witness the end of today, die now! in the name of Jesus.

- Situations that led to my conception and are now working contrary to my destiny, die! in Jesus name.

- Program of darkness in my foundation, keeping me from progress and prosperity die! in Jesus name.

- Anchor of sin that my foundation has planted in my life to waste my life, die, in the name of Jesus.

- Yokes of darkness suffocating and frustrating my destiny, die, in the name of Jesus.

- Bondages in my life arising from the wickedness of those familiar with me, die! in the name of Jesus.

- Every soul-tie established in the mind of whosoever is familiar with me to block my progress and breakthroughs, perish forever, in the name of Jesus.

- Ancestral vultures waiting for my unguarded hour to strike, die! in the name of Jesus.

- Ancestral Serpents and scorpions waiting

for my unguarded hour to bite, bite yourself to death, in the name of Jesus.

- Evil family pattern blocking my breakthroughs, die, in the name of Jesus.

- Evil family pattern from my father's house blocking my breakthroughs die, in the name of Jesus.

- Powers that manipulated my glory during birth and are still operating in my life, die! in Jesus name.

- Wicked powers waiting patiently to disgrace me, be disgraced to death, in the name of Jesus.

- Every blockage to my breakthrough originating from past sexual sins take the sacrifice of Christ and disappear, in the name of Jesus.

(2kings 9)
- Domestic witchcraft, parental witchcraft, polygamous witchcraft, parent-in-law witchcraft, strange children witchcraft die! in the name of Jesus.

- As Jezebel was thrown down to death, every spirit of witchcraft behind my case be thrown down to death now, in the name of Jesus.

- By the spirit of Jehu, I command to be thrown down to death, every witchcraft power assigned to paralyze me, in the name of Jesus.

- The spirit of catch and destroy, is the spirit of Jehu; Spirit of Jehu catch and destroy now the Jezebels in my life, in the name of Jesus.

- Anything or any presence that came into me when I was a baby to waste my life, hear the word of the Lord, come out, die and enter no more, in the name of Jesus.

- Wicked powers assigned to kill the helper in my spouse, die, in the name of Jesus.

- Wicked powers assigned to kill the helper in my children, die, in the name of Jesus.

- Evil dedication from body incisions, take the blood of Jesus and die, in the name of Jesus.

- Sacrifices I offered in the past and are still standing to work against me, die, in the name of Jesus.

- Evil altars left standing from evil sacrifices of the past, die, in the name of Jesus.

- Every evil sacrifice of the past still active to work against me, lose your power, in the name of Jesus.

- Every spirit wife that has made me a husband by evil laws, I am not your husband, perish with your laws, in the name of Jesus.

- Yokes, curses, anointing, bondages and strongholds of gather and scatter, die! in the name of Jesus.

- Powers troubling my hands in order to scatter where I gather, die, in the name of Jesus.

- Uproars of polygamous witchcraft from my Father's house, die, in name Jesus.

- Wicked powers from my father's house behind the uproar of darkness in my life perish, in the name of Jesus.

- Powers of the grave swallowing my helpers, die, in Jesus name

Eccl.3:1   Unto every thing, there is a season....
Job 39:2 Canst thou number the months that they fulfill or knowest thou the time they bring forth

- Lord, I yield my life to your purpose for my

life for the day, week and month and year, in the name of Jesus.

(Job 33:18 ...that he may withdraw man from his purpose)

- Powers secretly and cleverly stealing from me in order to impose poverty upon my life, die, in the name of Jesus.

- Satanic manipulation of my voice that will not allow my helpers to recognize my voice, die, in the name of Jesus.

- If my capacity to capture my helper's attention has been damaged, Holy Spirit restore it now, in the name of Jesus.

- If my capacity to capture my helper's attention has been satanically manipulated, Holy Spirit repair it now, in the name of Jesus.

- If my look, voice and presence have been satanically manipulated to confuse my divine helper, blood of Jesus incubate me for repair, in the name of Jesus.

CHAPTER 11

Command the Seventh Month: July

4 And the ark rested in the seventh month, on the seventeenth day of the month, upon the mountains of Ararat. 5 And the waters decreased continually until the tenth month: in the tenth month, on the first day of the month, were the tops of the mountains seen.
Gen 8:4-5 (KJV)

July is the seventh month of the year in the Julian and Gregorian Calendars and one of seven months with the length of 31 days.
Previously, it was called Quintilis in Latin, since it was the fifth month in the ancient Roman calendar, which traditionally set March as the beginning of the year before it was changed to January at the time of the decemvirs about 450 BC. The name was then changed by Augustus to honor Julius Caesar who

was born in July. In the ancient Roman calendar the ides of July fell on the 15th day of the month.

July starts on the same day of the week as April every year, and January in leap years. In a common year no other month ends on the same day as July, while in a leap year July ends on the same day of the week as January.

SPIRITUAL SIGNIFICANCE OF SEVEN

We come now to the great number of spiritual perfection. A number which, therefore, occupies so large a place in the works, and especially in the Word of God as being inspired by the Holy Spirit.

It is seven, therefore, that stamps with perfection and completeness that in connection with which it is used. Of time, it tells of the Sabbath, and marks off the week of seven days, which, artificial as it may seem to be, is universal and immemorial in its observance amongst all nations and in all times. It tells of that eternal Sabbath-keeping which remains for the people of God in all its everlasting perfection.

In the creative works of God, seven completes the colors of the spectrum and rainbow, and satisfies in music the notes of the scale. In each of these the eighth is only a repetition of the first. (E.W. Bullinger)

Why is dedication of July to Julio, the emperor of Roman empire?

July is the seventh month of the year. The ordinal

and numerical position is a perfect position spiritually. The figure seven in the spirit stands for perfection. The intrinsic qualities of perfection can be easily invoked for good and evil. The stamp of darkness on the seventh month is unmistakably clear in the dedication of the month to the spiritual entities symbolized by the throne of Rome. The throne and its derived powers are highly spiritual. The bible speaks of the prince of Persia, the prince of Greece as examples of spiritual entities, ancestral spirits behind the thrones of these nations.

Every throne and stool are backed by ancestral spirits who lends power to these thrones and stools. When the human occupants of these thrones are revered, the ancestral spirits behind them are revered. In fact, the coronation rites to these thrones always include an evil spiritual marriage ceremony, by which the human occupant of the throne is officially and spiritually married to the ancestral spirits behind the thrones. Case in point the Daijosal ceremony during the coronation rites of the Emperor of Japan.

The thrones and stools of every land, are in fact nothing but altars that makes those sitting on them living sacrifice- an element of worship to the ancestral spirits unto whom the thrones and stools are dedicated. The thrones and stools are dedicated altars! National altars! The power of a throne is the power of an altar! The month of July is dedicated to the roman emperor Julio, and invariably to the ancestral spirits behind the throne of the roman empire. The "Prince of Rome". The gods of the nation of Rome. The mere mention of the name of the month, is an element of worship to these gods. Alas, is that not all they want? To take the worship of man. To divert the worship man gives to the Most High, to themselves.

Any power secretly and cleverly demanding for my worship, hear me and hear me well, I worship only Christ, leave my worship alone and die! in the name of Jesus Christ

"And for this reason, the man shall leave his mother and father and cleave to his wife and the two shall become one." The evil spiritual marriage between the human occupant of the throne and the ancestral spirits behind the throne makes them one. Every subject, every citizen of the domain of that throne are also invariably drawn into this evil spiritual marriage unity. it is a unity with darkness and of darkness. The glories of the citizens are attached to the throne. No subject is allowed to rise above the throne. Hence the rite of shaving of the citizenry as part of coronation rites and ceremonies. Case in point, the throne of Edo Kingdom, in Midwestern Nigeria, West Africa. Shout this decree

By the power of Christ I break every link and attachment between my glory and the throne and stool of my place of birth and place of origin and place of residence, in the name of Jesus.

Mass enslavement and bewitchment is the strategy.

Shout again !

Every bewitchment and mind enslavement originating from the throne or stool of my place of origin, birth, and residence, to waste my life, die! in the name of Jesus.

Genesis 2:1-3 1 Thus the heavens and the earth were finished, and all the host of them. 2 And on the seventh day God ended his work which he had made; and he rested on the seventh day from all his work which he had made. 3 And God blessed the seventh day, and sanctified it: because that in it he had rested from all his work which God created and made.

The seventh day is Sabbath. Created before the fall of man, the Sabbath goes to show that time can be set apart and set aside for a specific purpose. Any attempt to employ time for any other purpose than that intended and specified would meet with repercussion. See Exodus 31:15

Six days may work be done; but in the seventh [is] the sabbath of rest, holy to the LORD: whosoever doeth [any] work in the sabbath day, he shall surely be put to death.

God takes the issue of the time dedicated to him very serious, at least serious enough to warrant death penalty for violation. Lets take a quick look at another scripture that depicts the power of dedicated time in the book of Nehemiah.

Neh.8:9 Then Nehemiah the governor, Ezra the priest and scribe, and the Levites who were instructing the people said to them all, "_This day is sacred to the LORD your God. Do not mourn or weep._" For all the people had been weeping as they listened to the words of the Law.

The day sacred to the Lord is dedicated to the Lord and cannot be used for what the Lord has not prescribed. You cannot mourn nor weep in the day dedicated to God. By the same token, the gods of the nations take days and months as sacred to themselves, dedicated to themselves and thereby render it unavailable to man to use for his own pleasure. The gods we served before coming to Christ by having certain times dedicated to themselves now determine when the new yam, or harvest can be eaten, when to fetch water from the river without getting hurt, when you can cross the river with no danger, when you can sing or play music. A brother told me that in Ghana, in some period of the year you cannot play music publicly or make unnecessary noise. That time is dedicated to the gods of the land.

The days of the week that are not available to me for progress and prosperity because they have been dedicated to the gods that are not Christ, become available by the power of Christ.

There are many kinds of calendars in use all over the world today. The calendar is very important and so important that the Almighty saw it fit to change the calendar of the children of Israel as they were about to leave Egypt.

Exodus 12:2 "This month [shall be] unto you the beginning of months: it [shall be] the first month of the year to you.

A calendar is a product of agreement, a product of a covenant! Every one that uses the calendar is a subscriber to the covenant that established the calendar. Your usage automatically subscribes you. What a mass membership! But we all subscribe to certain covenants in life without understanding the "fine print", the requirements of the covenant and by so doing the enemy is cashing on our ignorance. As you go through this book I speak into your life, that the ignorance that has wasted you this far shall be divinely replaced with divine knowledge, in the name of Jesus.

- If I am ignorantly subscribing to any covenant that is damaging to my destiny, I unsubscribe by fire! in the name of Jesus.

- Any covenant in my blood calling me a covenant violator, take the sacrifice of Christ and be silenced forever, in the name of Jesus.

- As a Priest and a King in Christ, ordained by God to rule here on earth, I tender the sacrifice of Christ to undo every dedication of the month of July and I rededicate the seventh month to Christ for divine worship, fellowship and communion, for progress, healing, success, promotion, prosperity and favor, in the name of Jesus.

- I reject every demand of worship made of me before the time of the month of July can be made available to me for progress and prosperity, in the name of Jesus.

- The God that has done it all for me, January to July, I acknowledge you, I bless you and I thank you, in the name of Jesus.

- Every transaction of the year required for my prosperity and greatness, O Lord God my Father, use the seventh month of perfection to perfect it in the name of Jesus Christ.

- Every transaction of the year required for my healing and miracle, O Lord God my Father, use the seventh month of perfection to perfect it in the name of Jesus Christ.

- Every transaction of the year required for the prosperity of my business and career, O Lord God my Father, use the seventh month of perfection to perfect it in the name of Jesus Christ.

- On the seventh day of creation, God rested.

This is the seventh month, O Lord give me rest from every unprofitable labor, in Jesus name

- ....from every unnecessary struggle, in Jesus name

- Holy Spirit disallow every evil wish of household wickedness for the month of July, in Jesus name.

- O God that disappoints the devices of the crafty so that their hands cannot preform their evil enterprise, disappoint the devices of household wickedness for the month of July, in Jesus name.

- O God that disappoints the devices of the crafty so that their hands cannot preform their evil enterprise, disappoint the devices of envious and hateful associates for the month of July, in Jesus name.

- Thou power of God that sets the 7th day apart for rest, set the seventh month apart for my dumbfounding breakthroughs, for my healing, for my promotion, in Jesus name.

- Evil demands of the gods unto whom July has been dedicated, take the sacrifice of Christ and expire now, for I am in Christ.

- Sacrificial demands of the gods unto whom July has been dedicated, I am above you in Christ, expire, in the name of Jesus.

****

A MUST FOR JULY.
Mystery of Rest from Ongoing Battles!
One full hour of praise @ the midnight gate preferably Saturday to Sunday all through the Month of July. The month of Perfect Rest and Perfection.
Read Psalm 69 (The Message Version)
Make 3 request of rest from specific ongoing battles in your life using a decree like below:

- O Lord God my Father, You gave the Sabbath-Rest as an ordinance forever, give me rest from this battle of "start well and finish poorly", in the name of Jesus.

- ...this battle of marital turbulence and failure....this battle of repeated loss of good jobs....this battle of prolonged singleness and loneliness.....this battle of barrenness...this curse of profitless hard labor..this curse of "you shall never make it"...this curse of "you shall never excel", in the mighty name of Jesus Christ

- Every good thing the evil dedication of the month of July has been programmed to steal or destroy in my life, take the power of Christ and become untouchable, in the name of Jesus.

- I cut off every influence of my past on the breakthroughs of July, in Jesus name.

- I break every curse of illegitimacy arising from the way my parents met each other, in Jesus name.

- Every curse that is making me to start well and finish poorly break! in Jesus name.

- Every curse of good start and poor finishing upon my destiny, break! in the name of Jesus.

- Every power of bad news, of tragedy and sorrow assigned against me in the month of July, backfire! in the name of Jesus

- Every concluded wickedness responsible for what I am going through, die and backfire, in the name of Jesus.

- Every concluded wickedness that I have not been able to avoid, I take refuge in Christ and demand divine substitution, in the name of Jesus.

- Every decided and concluded wickedness that has prospered against me, expire in the name of Jesus.

- Every concluded wickedness that has prospered against my star, marriage, ministry, finances and calling, die, in the name of Jesus.

- Holy Spirit increase my capacity to comprehend your communications, in the name of Jesus.

- I tender the sacrifice of Christ to satisfy every demand of the law keeping me where I do not belong, in Jesus name.

- I tender the sacrifice of Christ to satisfy every demand of the law imposing barrenness upon my life, body and marriage, in Jesus name.

- ...the law penalizing me of unpaid vow, dowry, in Jesus name.

- Powers waiting to use sex as an altar to sacrifice my breakthroughs, blessings, my progress in life, die suddenly in the name of Jesus.

- Payment of a demonic dowry that has initiated me into covenant I cannot fulfill, take the sacrifice of Christ and lose your power over my life, progress and marriage, in Jesus name.

- Evil spiritual marriage yoking me to the power that makes the good things in my life to end badly, be dissolved by the power in the blood of

Jesus, in the name of Jesus.

- I am yoked to Christ, every yoke to idols of my father's house break now! in the name of Jesus.

- The power that is making the good things in my life to end badly and has become a spirit wife in my life for that purpose, die by fire, in the name of Jesus.

- Powers making my problems to defy solutions by becoming a spirit spouse enforcing the problems in my life, die, in the name of Jesus.

- Properties of stubborn pursuer in my possession, that is making the pursuer to pursue me catch fire! in the name of Jesus.

- Properties of the stubborn pursuer I have inherited but I know nothing about, I give it up! in the name of Jesus.

- Every inherited battle making my situation to defy solution, take the sacrifice of Christ and expire! in Jesus name.

- Strange altars using strange methods to demand for my blood and shed my blood, scatter in the name of Jesus.

- Bondages transferred into my life on my day of birth by the very first hands that touched me, I am now in Christ, die out of my life, in the name of Jesus.

- Ancestral spirits claiming to have been neglected and offended and are now attacking me, be attacked by the warriors of heaven and die, in the name of Jesus.

- Ancestral spirits pursuing me for un-offered sacrifice and are now attacking me with poverty, sickness, failure and rejection, be attacked by the warriors of heaven in the name of Jesus.

- It is written, "Worship the Lord your God, and serve Him only", ancestral spirits pursuing me for worship, collide with the Rock of Ages and die, in the name of Jesus.

- Unpleasant situations in my life, marriage, career maintained by ancestral spirits, take the sacrifice of Christ and die, in the name of Jesus.

- Unpleasant situations generating fear to waste my life, I am in Christ, expire! in the name of Jesus.

- Bondages of darkness kept in place by the

ancestral spirits of my father's house, die, in the name of Jesus.

- Every ancestral spirit calling me husband, I am not your husband, I am married to Christ, fall down and die! in the name of Jesus.

CHAPTER 12

Command the Eighth Month: August

In the eighth month, in the second year of Darius, came the word of the LORD unto Zechariah, the son of Berechiah, the son of Iddo the prophet, saying Zech.1:1

As a priest and a king in Christ Jesus, I tender the sacrifice of Christ to undo every evil dedication of the month of August to idols and i rededicate the month to Christ for divine worship, divine fellowship and divine communion in the name of Jesus.

If I am approaching the gate of the month of August with the wrong garment, robe of righteousness of Christ replace my garment, In the name of Jesus

O gate of the month of August, hear the word of the Lord, I am in Christ and Christ is approaching with me, lift up your head, in the name of Jesus.

The eight month of the Gregorian calendar is dedicated to Augustus Caesar, the emperor of Rome. The dedication, in the spiritual sense, is not to the person Augustus Caesar, but to the ancestral spirit occupying the throne of the roman empire through Augustus Caesar. The occupant of the national altar of the roman empire. At the mention and writing of the name August, this demon takes worship. Every acknowledgement of the name is an act of worship.

The throne of Rome, the altar of Rome succeeded in taking two out of 12 months by dedication having inspired the creation and commissioning of the calendar. The two months with the highest number of births along with September.

SPIRITUAL SIGNIFICANCE OF EIGHT
It is 7 plus 1. Hence it is the number specially associated with Resurrection and Regeneration, and the beginning of a new era or order.
When the whole earth was covered with the flood, it was Noah "the eighth person" (2 Peter 2:5) who stepped out on to a new earth to commence a new order of things. "Eight souls" (1 Peter 3:20) passed through it with him to the new or regenerated world. Hence, too, circumcision was to be performed on the

eighth day (Gen 17:12), because it was the foreshadowing of the true circumcision of the heart, that which was to be "made without hands," even "the putting off of the body of the sins of the flesh by the circumcision of Christ" (Col 2:11). This is connected with the new creation.
The first-born was to be given to Jehovah on the eighth day (Exo 22:29,30).

The right prayers must always be used to address the idolatrous root of August. Decrees about the month, in order to be effective must deal with the tools and weapons the enemy employs to steal, kill and destroy. The weapons are always altars, evil covenants, evil sacrifices, gates, evil dedications, curses, foundation and gods. Manipulation is the driving force behind the transactions of the kingdom of darkness, just as love is for the kingdom of light. The time of August is not available for destiny fulfillment for those who cannot command the month of August. The availability of time for destiny fulfillment is a hoarded commodity under the grip of the enemy. He releases it to those who can be manipulated into giving him worship by sacrifice.

Power of un-offered satanic sacrifice assigned to deprive me of time for destiny fulfillment in August, die in the name of Jesus.

Dedication-revoking decrees are highly required if the month is to yield to you your portion. The economy of the kingdom of darkness has been so satanically arranged and ordered such that only those who understand the manipulative undertone can "prosper" within it. Those called out by Christ through salvation are however still being pursued just that they may be dispossessed of what Christ has procured for them on the cross of Calvary. The same way and manner the Israelites were pursued by Pharaoh even though they were being led out a pillar of cloud by day and a pillar of fire by night, the Most High himself. Being saved does not exempt you from the ongoing battles, it only empowers you to win the battles, if you diligently apply yourself. So in the light of this background how do we war to ensure victory?

If you are not saved, get into a relationship first of all before you can command the month. See opening prayers again otherwise you will be treated as an escapee or runaway slave by the kingdom of darkness to which you rightly belong until called out by grace. The lot of the escapee is terrible! This is the reason many complain of increased attacks the more they pray! Except Christ comes to you and call you out, it is almost, if not purely suicidal, to make a run away from your boss, Lucifer. He does not let go of his prisoners. "But shall the prey be taken from the mighty or the lawful captive delivered...?" Isaiah 49:24.

The moon god, unto whom the second day (Moon day or Monday) of the week is dedicated stands alongside with the ancestral spirit Augustus Caesar, the prince of Rome, at the gate of August 2011 to usher into the month and they have requirements. Just like the god of iron in the pantheon of the Yorubas of west Africa can only be worshipped with the blood of the dog, the gods have their individual requirements and preferences. The moon god and the prince of Rome (Remember the bible speaks of the prince of Persia and the prince of Greece) occupies the threshold altar of the month of August 2011. Evil covenants established this demon as overseer of the second day of the week just like the evil covenants that established the prince of Rome as the overseer of the month of August. But the issue of covenants has been settled for those who are in Christ. The covenant of the blood of Jesus overrides and overrules any other covenant.

- *Covenant of the blood of Jesus undo now every evil covenant that has been instituted over the month of August to render it unavailable for my breakthroughs, in the name of Jesus.*

- *Every grip of evil covenants on the time of August for my sake, the sake of my marriage and career, break ! in the name of Jesus.*

- *Satanic covenants rendering the month of August unavailable for my breakthroughs, die, in the name of Jesus.*

- *Holy Spirit take the time of this month out of*

darkness and ordain it for my breakthroughs in the name of Jesus. (..my marital breakthroughs, financial breakthroughs....etc), in the name of Jesus

- *I take the voice of Christ and I command the month of August to allow and witness the manifestation of the glory of God upon my life, in the name of Jesus*

...the manifestation of my breakthroughs
...the manifestation of my season of dance and laughter

- *Festivals and feasts of the month of August of my place of birth, assigned to renew and maintain old membership of evil covenants, I am now a member of the covenant of the blood of Jesus, exclude me and my household by fire!, in the name of Jesus*

- *Festivals and feasts of the month of August of my place of origin, assigned to renew old membership of evil covenants, I am now a member of the covenant of the blood of Jesus, exclude me and my household by fire!, in the name of Jesus*

- *Festivals and feasts of the month of August of my place of residence, assigned to renew and maintain old membership of evil covenants, I am now a member of the covenant of the blood of Jesus, exclude me and my household by fire!, in the name of Jesus*

- *Power of un-offered satanic sacrifice on the rampage in the month of August, I am in Christ, die !, in the name of Jesus*

- *Dark dedications of the month of August demanding for worship by sacrifice before I can excel and prosper, take the sacrifice of Christ and lose your power, in the name of Jesus*

- *Sacrificial demands of evil altars of the month of August arresting my progress, lose your power and let me prosper.*

- *If the month of August has been made unavailable for my progress and prosperity, Thou power of God make it available now! In the name of Jesus.*

- *Sacrificial demands of the dark dedications of the month holding onto my breakthroughs, healing, promotion, prosperity, take the valid payment of the sacrifice of Christ and let go!, in the name of Jesus*

- *womb of August, you are the womb of*

regeneration, resurrection, restoration and new beginning. Every good thing I have lost since my conception, O womb of August take on the power of Christ and reproduce now by miracle, in the name of Jesus

SPIRITUAL SIGNIFICANCE OF EIGHT
The spiritual significance of the number eight, the number of ordinal position of the month of August. Eight as a numeral is the superabundant number. It is 7 plus 1. Hence it is the number specially associated with Resurrection and Regeneration, and the beginning of a new era or order. As seven was so called because the seventh day was the day of completion and rest, so eight, as the eighth day, was over and above this perfect completion, and was indeed the first of a new series, as well as being the eighth. Thus it already represents two numbers in one, the first and eighth.

Scriptural transactions of the eighth month.
There are transactions in scripture that reflects the mind and time of the Almighty. These transactions can serve as basis of communication with the Divine. Seeing He permitted these transactions, He that changes not, who was, is, is to come, can do it again. We applaud God when we remember his goodness in the past. It is parallel to what the lawyers do in the court of law with legal precedents. The God that has done it before, do it again!

In the eighth month, in the second year of Darius, came the word of the LORD unto Zechariah, the son of Berechiah, the son of Iddo the prophet, saying Zech.1:1

The transaction of Zechariah 1.1 is transaction useful for those who want to hear from God. Those who need revelation of secrets. Those who need to hear God speak.

It was in the eighth month the Lord spoke to Zechariah. This is the eighth month, Holy Spirit speak to me, in the name of Jesus

1 King 6:37 The foundation of the temple of the LORD was laid in the fourth year, in the month of Ziv. 38 In the eleventh year in the month of Bul, the eighth month, the temple was finished in all its details according to its specifications. He had spent seven years building it.

Good projects of my life that have refused to positively conclude, hear the word of the Lord, as the temple of the Lord was finished in all its details in the eighth month, positively and favorably conclude now, this is the eighth month, in the name of Jesus.

Command the Month @ the Midnight Gate

CHAPTER 13

Command the Ninth Month: September

Jeremiah 36:9 In the ninth month of the fifth year of Jehoiakim son of Josiah king of Judah, a time of fasting before the LORD was proclaimed for all the people in Jerusalem and those who had come from the towns of Judah.

September as the ninth month is the month of conclusion, finality and judgment.

In Latin, septem means "seven" and septimus means "seventh"; September was in fact the seventh month of the Roman calendar until 153 BC, when the first month changed from Kalendas Martius (1 March) to Kalendas Januarius (1 January). It is also the seventh month of the Astrological calendar, which begins with March/Mars/Aries. No other month ends on the same day of the week as September in any year. (Wikipedia)

SPIRITUAL SIGNIFICANCE OF NINE

The number nine is a most remarkable number in many respects. It is held in great reverence by all who study the occult sciences; and in mathematical science it possesses properties and powers which are found in no other number.* It is the last of the digits, and thus marks the end; and is significant of the conclusion of a matter. It is akin to the number six, six being the sum of its factors (3x3=9, and 3+3=6), and is thus significant of the end of man, and the summation of all man's works. Nine is, therefore, the number of finality and judgment, for judgment is committed unto Jesus as "the Son of man" (John 5:27; Acts 17:31). It marks the completeness, the end and issue of all things as to man—the judgment of man and all his works.

It is a factor of 666, which is 9 times 74. (E.W Bullinger)

The Secrets of the ....ember Months

The names of the last four months of the year bear no resemblance to their ordinal position in the calendar. This is a deliberate transaction of darkness to confuse and deceive. If proper identification is required for a victory in spiritual warfare, you are made to start on the wrong foot by addressing the ninth month with the appellation of the seventh. You may think there is nothing wrong to address the ninth month as the seventh so long we all agreed to do so. But remember the origin of the inspiration that established it. The enemy does nothing without a reason.

The last four months of the year all end in -ember because they have taken after their numerical position albeit in a period when the calendar had ten months. The enemy is never without a plan. The satanic quota that must be fulfilled before the end of the year has informed this strategy of mis-identification or improper identification. When you speak concerning September that means the seventh, the ninth month would feel unaddressed, preempting your decrees. In the warfare over time, you would do well to properly refer to September as the ninth month.

- *Ninth month by name September, reject satanic agenda programmed into you for my sake, in the name of Jesus.*

- *Ninth month by name September, if you are under demonic enchantment for my sake, I break the enchantment by the power in the blood of Jesus.*

- *Whenever I refer to September, O ninth month answer me! in Jesus name.*

- *It is the truth that digits double after nine!*

As the digits double up after nine, let my blessings of the ninth month double up hereafter in the name of Jesus.

- *Every spirit spouse that has chosen September to enter into my life, die before you do so, in the name of Jesus.*

- *Spirit spouse ruling me from my eyes, I have possessed the eyes of Christ, die! in the name of Jesus.*

- *Spirit spouse ruling me from my head, ears, mouth, nose, hands, feet, reproductive organs, organs in my body, I am now in Christ, die! in the name of Jesus.*

- *Every evil spiritual marriage I have entered into by the incisions and marks on my face and body, be dissolved now, I am married to Christ, in the name of Jesus.*

- *Any power waiting to destroy me when I get to the top, die before I get there! in the name of Jesus.*

- *In the dream and mind of my helpers, my picture appear and remain until I am helped! in the name of Jesus.*

- *In the dream and mind of my divine helpers,*

thoughts of me appear and remain until I am helped, in the name of Jesus.

- *The thoughts of Mordecai appeared and remained in the mind of the King that he could not sleep. My helper, lose your sleep until you help me, In the name of Jesus.*

- *Divine favor and Divine Mercy locate me and remove every of garment of disfavor, hatred and rejection in the name of Jesus.*

- *Evil judgment to have me displaced from my place of glory and place of destiny, backfire! in the name of Jesus.*

- *Evil judgment exploiting my ignorance to get smuggled into my life, backfire and be overruled by the judgment of heaven, in the name of Jesus.*

- *Altars cooperating with any evil judgment ever passed or will be passed on me, be dismantled in the name of Jesus.*

- *Angels of frustration assigned to wear me out, return to your sender, in the name of Jesus.*

- *I release the power of the blood of Jesus to destroy every strange presence in my head, eyes, ears, mouth, nose and hands, in the name of Jesus.*

- *My hands, if you are following a satanic program to take me out of my place of destiny, I break the program, in the name of Jesus.*

- *My marital life, if you are following a satanic program of perpetual loneliness, I break the program! in the name of Jesus.*

- *My marriage, if you are following a satanic program of compulsory divorce, I break the program in the name of Jesus.*

- *Sacrifice required of me for any ritual-assisted healing of the past, lose your hold, I am now in Christ, In Jesus name.*

- *Sacrifice required of me because of any ritual-assisted deliverance of the past, I tender the sacrifice of Christ, lose your hold, in the name of Jesus.*

- *Every satanic decision ensuring that I will not prosper coming to Christ, I overthrow you in the name of Jesus.*

- *Signs of the times not in my favor in the ninth month, expire and perish by the blood of Jesus. (Matt. 16:3)*

- *Every bondage in my waist, die! in the name of Jesus.*

- *Strange powers occupying my waist, die! in the name of Jesus.*

- *Concluded wickedness of the ninth day of the ninth month, I am not available, exclude me and my household in the name of Jesus.*

- *Concluded wickedness of the ninth month targeted at my marriage, ministry and job, back to sender! in the name of Jesus.*

- *Every finalized evil judgment of the ninth day of the ninth month against my destiny, be undone by the power in the blood of Jesus.*

- *For every demand for payment for my sins, the sins of my parents, the sins of my ancestors, I tender the sacrifice of Christ as a valid payment, in the name of Jesus.*

- *Evil thoughts in the heart of those who do not wish me well that has become bewitching, perish ! in the name of Jesus.*

- *Power of discouragement and*

disappointment, die! in the name of Jesus.

- *11th day of the 9th month, if you have become an appointed time of darkness, of witchcraft, of tragedy, cease to be ! in the name of Jesus.*

- *Wicked powers that have chosen the 11th day of the ninth month as an appointed time of darkness for me and my household, fall down and die, in the name of Jesus.*

- *I take the power of Christ and I reverse every finalized wickedness of the 11th day of the 9th month, in the name of Jesus.*

- *Wicked powers Making my children my source of sorrow, die, in the name of Jesus.*

- *The gods calling me by crisis and with crisis, the Lord rebuke you! in the name of Jesus.*

- *The gods of my father's house using crisis to draw my attention and demand for my worship, the Lord rebuke you! in the name of Jesus.*

- *Anger, lust and pride that has become a power of "I can see it but I cannot have it," die! in the name of Jesus.*

.....I can have it but I cannot enjoy it
......this is how far I can go

- *The powers creating crisis in my life in order to demand for worship, perish with your demand, I worship only Christ, in the name of Jesus.*

- *Negative family anointing assigned to waste my calling, die, in the name of Jesus.*

- *Arrow of death and decay targeted at me backfire, in the name of Jesus.*

- *Foundational bondage and inherited troubles keeping me from my breakthroughs expire in the name of Jesus.*

- *Consequences of ancestral bondage, take the sacrifice of Christ and clear away by fire, in the name of Jesus.*

- *Every anointing of immorality flowing around in my foundation, stay out of my life and dry up by fire, in the name of Jesus*

- *Evil family pattern programed to appear in my life by my next birthday, fail to do so, in the name of Jesus.*

- *The hour of the power of darkness programed to appear in the ninth month, in this week, fail to do so, in the name of Jesus*

- *Brigade of Judas waiting for the dark hour to appear, scatter before the hour in the name of Jesus.*

- *Every foundational bondage originating from the immorality of my parents and ancestors, I am now in Christ, die in the name of Jesus.*

- *Everywhere my tradition has become evil gate for darkness, mercy of God in Christ shut the gate now. I subscribe to the traditions of the kingdom of God, in the name of Jesus.*

- *Customs of my father's house, tribe and nation, that has become an anchor of darkness, perish! in the name of Jesus.*

- *Anchors to darkness made out of the traditions and (customs) of my place of origin, I am now in Christ, break, in the name of Jesus.*

- *Agenda to steal from me this month, scatter! in the name of Jesus.*

- *Satanic siphons attached to my breakthroughs and benefits, die! in the name of Jesus.*

CHAPTER 14

Command the Tenth Month: October

4 And the ark rested in the seventh month, on the seventeenth day of the month, upon the mountains of Ararat. 5 And the waters decreased continually until the tenth month: in the tenth month, on the first day of the month, were the tops of the mountains seen.
Gen 8:4-5 (KJV)

1 In the tenth year, in the tenth month, in the twelfth day of the month, the word of the Lord came unto me, saying, 2 Son of man, set thy face against Pharaoh king of Egypt, and prophesy against him, and against all Egypt:
Ezek 29:1-2 (KJV)

October is the tenth month of the year in the Julian and Gregorian Calendars and one of seven months with a length of 31 days. The eighth month in the old Roman calendar, October retained its name (from the Latin "octo" meaning "eight") after January and February were inserted into the calendar that had originally been created by the Romans.
In the 19th century, the month of October was dedicated to the devotion of the rosary in Roman

Catholic countries.

Spiritual Significance of Ten
Ten is one of the perfect numbers, and signifies the perfection of Divine order, commencing, as it does, an altogether new series of numbers. The first decade is the representative of the whole numeral system, and originates the system of calculation called "decimals," because the whole system of numeration consists of so many tens, of which the first is a type of the whole.
Completeness of order, marking the entire round of anything, is, therefore, the ever-present signification of the number ten. It implies that nothing is wanting; that the number and order are perfect; that the whole cycle is complete.
NOAH completed the antediluvian age in the tenth generation from God.
THE TEN COMMANDMENTS contain all that is necessary, and no more than is necessary, both as to their number and their order, while THE LORD'S PRAYER is completed in ten clauses. (E.W. Bullinger)

Tenth month by name October, disobey satanic orders issued for my sake, the sake of my career and marital life/marriage, in the name of Jesus.

Tenth month by name October, whenever you are summoned to work against me, reject the summon, in the name of Jesus.

Every time I mention October, I refer to the tenth month and not the eight month as the name implies, in the name of Jesus.

Every evil spiritual marriage programmed to be celebrated in my life by this month, blood of Jesus disallow it, in the name of Jesus

....by the end of the year
...by my next birthday

- *Evil covenant approaching time of renewal this day, week and month, blood of Jesus break it now.*

- *In the tenth month, Ezekiel prophesied against Pharaoh and Egypt. Every Pharaoh pursuing me, i prophesy against you in the name of Jesus, this is the tenth month, in the name of Jesus.*

- *Spirit of masquerade, you are the spirit of evil competition and wickedness, die out of my life, in the name of Jesus.*

- *Evil dedication by incisions and marks, die! in the name of Jesus.*

- *Every evil demand for worship blocking my heavens, die! in the name of Jesus.*

- *Every evil demand for worship sabotaging my breakthroughs, die, in the name of Jesus.*

- *The power that enjoy to lust and is illegally married to me in the spirit, I divorce you, in the name of Jesus.*

- *Spirit of "it is not yet my turn" afflicted Rachel and took from her the position of the first wife; every spirit of "it is not yet my turn" assigned to frustrate me, die, in the name of Jesus.*

- *Every room I have given out of ignorance to the enemy to afflict me, I take it back! in the name of Jesus.*

- *Anything in my life cooperating with the devil, die! in the name of Jesus.*

- *I cancel the maturity date of any evil dream, in the name of Jesus.*

- *Every evil dedication maintained by the incisions, scars and marks on my face and body, take the blood of Jesus and die! in the name of Jesus.*

- *Evil spiritual marriage maintained by*

incisions, scars and marks on my body, scatter! in the name of Jesus.

- *Satanic authority maintaining affliction, sickness, disappointment in my life die, in the name of Jesus.*

- *Demons in my life by incisions, marks and tattoos, perish now! in the name of Jesus.*

- *Demons hiding in my body/ face, to lust, to get angry, to get proud, to get rebellious, die by fire, in the name of Jesus.*

- *Strangers hiding in my body/ face to lust, hear the word of the Lord, run out of your hiding place and enter no more! in the name of Jesus.*

- *Strangers in my body, face, hands, come out by fire! in the name of Jesus.*

- *Everything given to me for food in my dream and has become a demon in my body, die! in the name of Jesus.*

- *Acquired, transferred and inherited demons hiding in my body, face, hands, hear the word of the Lord, die! in Jesus name.*

- *Every evil spiritual marriage contorting my*

face, every evil spiritual marriage twisting my hands, every evil spiritual marriage arresting my feet,.. D I E ! in the name of Jesus.

- *Every evil spiritual marriage distorting my face, twisting my hands and arresting my feet, die! in the name of Jesus.*

Luke 10:19-20. I give you power ....spirits are subject to me....

- *It is written: spirits are subject to me, every contrary spirit hear me and hear me well, come out of your hiding place and enter no more, in the name of Jesus.*

Who shall deliver me from this body of death? A cry for deliverance by an apostle?

- *Every spiritual marriage that has twisted my look, my face, my body, and my life, die! in Jesus name.*

- *Consequences of incisions, marks and scars on my body, face and hands be reversed in the name of Jesus.*

- *Gates of sexual sin opened into my life by incisions and tattoos on my face, on my waist, on my body be shut down by fire, in* the name of Jesus

- It is written, it is not good for a man to be alone. Every loneliness in my life, come to an end now, in the name of Jesus.

- Spirit of "here I am send me" overtake me. Power of "Here I am send me" overwhelm me. Anointing of "here I am send me" fall on me, in the name of Jesus.

Ruth1: 15. ....her people and her gods.......
- The gods of my father's house, still on my pursuit, collide with the rock of ages and die! in the name of Jesus.

- Whosoever has taken my picture to on an evil altar, I command the picture to disappear, in the name of Jesus.

- My properties serving as evil point of contacts on satanic altars, catch fire, in the name of Jesus.

- Effects of evil hands that have ever touched my head, be removed, be washed off by the blood of Jesus, in the name Jesus.

- Effects of polluted hands that have ever touched my head, be removed by the blood of Jesus, in the name of Jesus.

- *Whosoever has been satanically anointed to disgrace me, lose the anointing by fire, in the name of Jesus.*

Ecc.9:11   I returned, and saw under the sun, that the race is not to the swift, nor the battle to the strong, neither yet bread to the wise, nor yet riches to men of understanding, nor yet favour to men of skill; but time and chance happeneth to them all. (Ecclesiastes 9:11 KJV)

- *Lord, use time and chance to favor me in my marriage , career, ministry, in the name of Jesus.*

- *Lord, use time and chance to locate my divine partner, in the name of Jesus.*

- *Every evil dedication that has imposed a strange look upon me, die! in the name of Jesus.*

- *Embargoed glories, hear the word of Christ! Arise! in the name of Jesus.*

- *Spiritually blind eyes, hear the word of Christ, Ephrata ! Open! in the name of Jesus.*

- *Eyes that are not human but are watching*

/monitoring, looking at me, receive blindness, in the name of Jesus.

- *Hands that touched me and are not human, but are agents of darkness, die with your effects.*

Your sorrow is ignited by your own thoughts…
- *Fear-producing thoughts, sorrow-producing thoughts, discouragement-producing thoughts assigned to kill my faith in God, die! in Jesus name.*

- *Satanic revocations of what the Lord has blessed me with, be undone in the name of Jesus.*

- *Satanic legal grounds depriving me of good things of life, ministry and marriage, take the sacrifice of Christ and die! in the name of Jesus.*

- *Satanic legal grounds that have deprived me of good things of life, marriage and career, die! in the name of Jesus.*

- *Legal grounds cobbled together to deprive me of what is rightly and legally mine, be nullified in the name of Jesus.*

- *Legal grounds put together to steal from me, to kill and destroy good things in my life, be nullified! in the name of Jesus.*

- *Any organ of my body on any evil altar catch fire! in the name of Jesus.*

CHAPTER 15

Command the Eleventh Month: November

2 (There are eleven days' journey from Horeb by the way of mount Seir unto Kadesh barnea.) 3 And it came to pass in the fortieth year, in the eleventh month, on the first day of the month, that Moses spake unto the children of Israel, according unto all that the Lord had given him in commandment unto them; 4 After he had slain Sihon the king of the Amorites, which dwelt in Heshbon, and Og the king of Bashan, which dwelt at Astaroth in Edrei: 5 On this side Jordan, in the land of Moab, began Moses to declare this law, saying, 6 The Lord our God spake unto us in Horeb, saying, Ye have dwelt long enough in this mount: 7 Turn you, and take your journey, and go to the mount of the Amorites, and unto all the places nigh thereunto, in the plain, in the hills, and in

the vale, and in the south, and by the sea side, to the land of the Canaanites, and unto Lebanon, unto the great river, the river Euphrates. 8 Behold, I have set the land before you: go in and possess the land which the Lord sware unto your fathers, Abraham, Isaac, and Jacob, to give unto them and to their seed after them.
Deut 1:2-8 (KJV)

November is the 11th month of the year in the Julian and Gregorian Calendars and one of four months with the length of 30 days. November was the ninth month of the ancient Roman calendar. November retained its name (from the Latin novem meaning "nine") when January and February were added to the Roman calendar.

Spiritual Significance: November
Though occupying the eleventh position, the name suggests ninth. Again the case of mis-identification. Eleven can be viewed as 10+1=11 or 12 -1=11. Both 10 and 12 are numbers that suggest completion and order. To alter that status quo is the story of 11. This is the reason why 11 stands for disorder, disorganization and disintegration. These qualities can be invoked wherever we have to to do with the number 11.

- **Halloween threshold transactions assigned to pollute my threshold, scatter!, in the name of Jesus**

- **Power of Halloween cauldrons assigned against me, die!, in the name of Jesus**

- **Evil covenants waiting to be renewed, so that bondages, afflictions in my life may be renewed, so that stubborn situations in my life may continue, fail to do so, in the name of Jesus**

- **Evil dedications and covenants waiting to be renewed during Halloween, fail to do so!, in the Jesus name of Jesus**

- **Halloween gifts assigned to renew evil covenants upon my land, my land of breakthrough, become of no effect, in the name of Jesus.**

- **Halloween foundation of disorder, disorganization and disintegration for the eleventh month , scatter!, in the name of Jesus**

- **Every anti-kingdom Halloween threshold transaction, scatter and backfire!, in the name of Jesus**

- **Every evil covenant that has been cut on my threshold through the exchange of halloween gifts break and die!, in the name** of Jesus

- Every affliction that has dwelt with me since the beginning of the year, enough is enough, come to an end!, in the name of Jesus

- Wicked powers invoking disorder and disorganization into my life in the eleventh month, I am in Christ, fail and die!, in the name of Jesus

- Satanic transactions of the eleventh month, designed to kill me before the end of the year, scatter, in the name of Jesus

- Every bird of darkness working against my progress in the eleventh month fall down and die, in the name of Jesus

- Any power assigned to use me as sacrifice in the eleventh month, die, in Jesus name

- Any power assigned to use me as Halloween sacrifice, die, in the name of Jesus.

- Eleventh month by name November, cooperate with my breakthroughs, healing, deliverance, restoration, recovery, in the name of Jesus

- As I approach the end of the year, spirit of sabbatical rest, fall upon me in the name of Jesus.

- I curse every local altar of the eleventh month fashioned against me, in the name of Jesus

- Every covenant with the earth against my life in the eleventh month, break, in Jesus name
  .....with sun, moon and stars
  ....with the moon

- In the eleventh month God regarded the affliction of Israel as too much and demanded for a reprieve! This is the eleventh month, O Lord, regard my troubles as too much and grant me a reprieve, in the name of Jesus. (Zechariah 1:13-15)

I will enter his gate with thanksgiving!

- As thanksgiving takes through the gate of the Divine, I give You thanks O Lord, to enter through the gate of the month and praise to prosper in the month, in the name of Jesus

- **As a sacrifice takes through the gate of the tabernacle, I tender the sacrifice of Christ to take me through the gate of breakthrough , healing, prosperity, deliverance in the eleventh month by name November, in the name of Jesus**

- **My presence at this midnight gate is a (my) token of seeking first the kingdom of God and it's righteousness. Every blessing and breakthrough that has been missing in my life, be added unto me now, in the name of Jesus.**

  ...deeper fear of God be added unto me, in Jesus name.

  …landmark healing be added unto me now! in Jesus name.

  ... deliverance from marine witchcraft, be added unto me in the name of Jesus.

  …deliverance from polygamous witchcraft, siblings witchcraft, envious associate witchcraft, demonic neighbor witchcraft, my father's house witchcraft be added unto me in the name of Jesus.

- **My Father, impute unto me the**

righteousness of Christ without measure ! in the name of Jesus.

- Whatsoever I am paying for that has necessitated my present situation of lack, loneliness, married but lonely, married and unhappy, divorce, sickness, mercy of God in Christ avail for me and change my story in the name of Jesus.

- Channels of communication between me and darkness, be permanently shut down, in the name of Jesus.

- Strange voices speaking confusion into my essence, my life, marriage, die! in the name of Jesus.

- Strange voices discouraging me from seeking first the kingdom of God and it's righteousness, be silenced by the blood of Jesus.

- Lord, let my thoughts, words and deeds minister unto You today!, in the name of Jesus.

- Lord, let the words of my mouth and the meditation of my heart be acceptable in thy sight, in the name of Jesus.

- Evil dedication of the day, week and month that is not allowing me a profitable use of the time of the day, week and month, die in the name of Jesus.

- Holy Spirit undo every evil dedication of the day, week and month programmed to rob me of a profitable use of my time, in the name of Jesus.

- If the time of this day, week and month is not available to me for prosperity, progress, breakthrough, peace, peace in marriage, happiness in marriage, fulfillment in marriage, marital breakthrough and success because of evil dedication, My Father break the dedication, in the name of Jesus.

- If the time of the day, week and month is not available to me for progress and prosperity because of evil dedication, blood of Jesus break the dedication, in the name of Jesus.

- .....is not available that my helpers may locate me, in Jesus name.

- If the time of the day, week and month is not available to me to seek first the kingdom of God and it's righteousness because of evil dedication, Holy Spirit break the dedication, in the name of Jesus.

- My Father, there are powers troubling my star, stop them before they stop me, in the name of Jesus.

- My Father there are satanic agents tormenting my life, stop them before they stop me, in the name of Jesus.

- Dark altars at the gate of the eleventh month assigned to steal from me in the eleventh month, collapse and die!, in the name of Jesus

- I employ the sacrifice of Christ to undo every evil dedication of the eleventh month by name November to the gods and idols of the nations, in the name of Jesus.

- I employ the sacrifice of Christ to dedicate this month to Christ to seek first the kingdom of God and his righteousness, in the name of Jesus.

    ...for divine worship, divine fellowship and divine communion, in Jesus name.

    ...for breakthroughs, healing, deliverance, in the name of Jesus.

- **Wherever I have been deceived into ungodly lifestyle, mercy of God in Christ arise and deliver me! in the name of Jesus.**

- **Every good thing I have been programmed never to achieve, as I am praying, come to past now! in the name of Jesus.**

CHAPTER 16

Command the Twelfth Month: December

27 And it came to pass in the seven and thirtieth year of the captivity of Jehoiachin king of Judah, in the twelfth month, on the seven and twentieth day of the month, that Evilmerodach king of Babylon in the year that he began to reign did lift up the head of Jehoiachin king of Judah out of prison; 28 And he spake kindly to him, and set his throne above the throne of the kings that were with him in Babylon; 29 And changed his prison garments: and he did eat bread continually before him all the days of his life. 30 And his allowance was a continual allowance given him of the king, a daily rate for every day, all the days of his life.
2 Kings 25:26-30 (KJV)

- **The head of the King rejected captivity in the 12th month. I am a priest and a King! My head reject every captivity of the 12th month, in the name of Jesus.**

13 And the letters were sent by posts into all the king's provinces, to destroy, to kill, and to cause to perish, all Jews, both young and old, little children and women, in one day, even upon the thirteenth day of the twelfth month, which is the month Adar, and to take the spoil of them for a prey.
Esther 3:13 (KJV)

11 Wherein the king granted the Jews which were in every city to gather themselves together, and to stand for their life, to destroy, to slay, and to cause to perish, all the power of the people and province that would assault them, both little ones and women, and to take the spoil of them for a prey, 12 Upon one day in all the provinces of king Ahasuerus, namely, upon the thirteenth day of the twelfth month, which is the month Adar. 13 The copy of the writing for a commandment to be given in every province was published unto all people, and that the Jews should be ready against that day to avenge themselves on their enemies
Esther 8:11-13 (KJV)

Esther 9:1 Now in the twelfth month, that is, the month Adar, on the thirteenth day of the same, when the king's commandment and his decree drew near to be put in execution, in the day that the enemies of the Jews hoped to have power over them, (though it was turned to the contrary, that the Jews had rule over them that hated them;) 2 The Jews gathered themselves together in their cities throughout all the provinces of the king Ahasuerus, to lay hand on such

as sought their hurt: and no man could withstand them; for the fear of them fell upon all people. 3 And all the rulers of the provinces, and the lieutenants, and the deputies, and officers of the king, helped the Jews; because the fear of Mordecai fell upon them. 4 For Mordecai was great in the king's house, and his fame went out throughout all the provinces: for this man Mordecai waxed greater and greater. 5 Thus the Jews smote all their enemies with the stroke of the sword, and slaughter, and destruction, and did what they would unto those that hated them.
Esther 9:1-5 (KJV)

- *As the story of the Jews changed for the best in the twelfth month, let my story change for the best, this is the twelfth month, in the name of Jesus.*

- *As the Jews could suffer no destruction in the twelfth month, I ....(mention your full name) will suffer no destruction, I am in the twelfth month, in the name of Jesus.*

- *Everything turned contrary for the enemies of the Jews in the twelfth month. Contrary wind! blow now on my enemies, this is the twelfth month, in the name of Jesus.*

- *The sadness and sorrow of the Jews became joy and gladness in the twelfth month, every sadness and sorrow in my life*

become joy and gladness, this is the twelfth month, in the name of Jesus.

December is the 12th and last month of the year in the Julian and Gregorian Calendars and one of seven months with the length of 31 days. December starts on the same day as September every year and ends on the same day as April every year. In Latin, decem means "ten". December was also the tenth month in the Roman calendar until a monthless winter period was divided between January and February.

The way and manner you end December will determine how you end the year and also how you start the new year and new month.
To end the twelfth month badly is to end the year badly and also start the new year and month badly! Many are too carried away by the idolatrous festivities of the season rather that interest themselves in this. Many are closing out the month and the year in depression and therefore starts the new year in depression. Of course, when the foundation is destroyed what can the righteous do? Where is the foundation of the new year? and the new month? Everything has a foundation! More so in the spirit.

The principle of laying a foundation is hidden in the principle of the Sabbath, which is a principle of rest.

The seventh day rest is closing out the old week and at the same time laying the foundation for the new week. The Sabbath was the last of God's seven-day creation. Though not a physical creation but a creation nonetheless. A Divine pattern! "See that you build it according to the pattern i showed you on the mount!"

According to pattern, one-seventh of the cycle time is required to keep the cycle functional, healthy, fulfilling and prosperous. The cycles of the week, the month and the year will be better off subscribing to this principle. Law of thermodynamics concords. "It is impossible to create a perpetual motion machine". It is impossible to be successful and fulfilled in the cycles without a one-seventh rest period.

Christ has fulfilled the requirements of the Sabbath. The perpetual toil to satisfy the divine requirements of the law, has ended with Christ payment. We can rest from that toil to satisfy God through the law. Our prayer, lifestyle, attitude and disposition must however reflect the principle of Sabbath. If we must pray according to the mind of God, then our prayers at this time of the year must show the principles of Sabbath. The Sabbath has become "spiritualized", in the same fashion blood sacrifice has become "spiritualized", still observed in principle and spirit, taking a reality in Christ. I am in Christ!

- **If I am approaching the end of the year without rest in my spirit and attitude, Christ** my Sabbath, become rest in my body, soul, spirit and attitude, in the name of Jesus.

- **Foundation-laying transactions, that would ensure monumental progress in the new month and year, come into place now, by the power of the sacrifice of Christ, in the name of Jesus.**

- **Purpose of God for my life in the approaching month and year, i initiate your foundation in this last month of the year on the blood of Jesus and the glory of the Living God, in the name of Jesus.**

- **My breakthroughs of next year, I lay your foundation now on the sure Rock that is Christ! in the name of Jesus**

The December closure/January opening Gate is a highly important gate because you can get to multi-transact. From the most basic of cycle of time to the greatest cycle of time can be effectively addressed from this one gate. Not only could you speak to the gate of the day, weeks, months and year, where applicable you can speak to the gate of a decade, century and even millennium! You can set the tone of each of these cycles from this one gate.

- **Requirements for prosperous entry through**

the gate of the new year and month, take the sacrifice of Christ and be fulfilled! in the name of Jesus

- Holy Spirit empower me to live out the sufficiency of Christ, no matter what! in the name of Jesus

- Holy Spirit empower me with the sacrifice required for a successful and prosperous entry into the next year, in the name of Jesus.

- Every deadline of time set up to wear me out and make me run helter-skelter, expire in the name of Jesus.

- Deadline set up by my age, hear the word of the Lord, by the spirit of Sarah, that does not pay attention to age, I overcome you, in the name of Jesus.

- By the spirit of Sarah that pays no attention to age, I overcome every deadline set up using my age to wear me out, in the name of Jesus.

- Any power using my age as a deadline to wear me out, die! in the name of Jesus.

- The evil covenant of my father's house that

I have violated by coming to Christ and its now punishing me for coming to Christ, take the blood of Jesus and die, in the name of Jesus.

- Abraham gave up Isaac and became father of many nations. All I need to give up for my next level to manifest, I give it up in Christ, in the name of Jesus.

- The summon I responded to and it's manipulating my glory, backfire with visible evidence, in the name of Jesus.

- Evil covenants that my coming to Christ have violated, and are now punishing me, take the sacrifice of Christ and die, in the name of Jesus.

- My blood reject evil communications, in Jesus name.

Heb.8:9 not like the covenant that I made with their fathers
on the day when I took them by the hand to bring them out of the land of Egypt.

- Lord, You took Israel by the hand out of Egypt. Take me by the hand out of this year into next year, in the name of Jesus.

- The God that took Israel by the hand out of bondage, take me by the hand out of this stubborn situation of shame and disgrace, in the name of Jesus.

- ...take me out of every situation wasting my life, in the name of Jesus.

- Lord, you took Israel by the hand to bring them out of Egypt, take me by the hand to bring me out of my predicament, out of this stubborn situation, in the name of Jesus.

- The hand of God that led Israel out of Egypt lead me out of every stubborn situation,..... unprofitable relationship, in the name of Jesus.

- Requirements for my prosperity in the next year, that are still in this year, gather yourself together and come with me as i move into the next year, in the name of Jesus.

- The gods that my coming to Christ has troubled and are now pursuing me, collide with the Rock of Ages and die! in Jesus name.

- As the new covenant replaced the old covenant, covenant of the blood of Jesus, replace every covenant dedicating this day to the gods of the nations, in the name of Jesus.

- The gates of my father's house that have predetermined how far I can go in life, I no longer subscribe to you. I subscribe to the gate that is Christ, in the name of Jesus.

- The gates of my place of origin that are remote controlling the kind of breakthroughs the indigenes can receive, count me out, I am now in Christ, in the of name of Jesus.

- Twelfth month by name December, hear me and hear me well, before you come to an end give me my portion, in the name of Jesus.

- Lord my God let me be fruitful in every good work I do, in the name of Jesus.

- As Mordecai was not disappointed in the 12th month this is the 12th month I will not be disappointed in the name of Jesus. (Esther 3:7)

- As the attack against Mordecai backfired in the 12th month every attack against me backfire, this is the 12th month. (Esther

3:13)

- **Every plan to have me slaughtered without mercy, this is the 12th month, you shall not prosper!, in the name of Jesus.**

- **Every power that is waiting to seize my belonging and spoil me in the 12th month, you are a liar, die!, in the name of Jesus.**

- **As the Jews had rule over those that hated them in the 12th month I shall have rule over those who hate me in this 12th month, in the name of Jesus.**

- **As the Jews triumphed over their enemies in the 12th month, this is the 12th month I shall triumph over my stubborn pursuers (Esther 12:1), in the name of Jesus.**

- **Any prison of darkness assigned to hold me captive, this is the 12th month! release me now!, in the name of Jesus.**

- **Every dream of darkness that is negatively affecting my marital destiny backfire! in the name of Jesus.**

- **Any power that is manipulating evil unto my marriage fall down and die!**

- **Any evil habit handed over to me in a dream to destroy my marital life backfire, in the name of Jesus.**

- **Any power that wants to draw me into an evil marriage in the dream die with your marriage, in the name of Jesus.**

- **I reject, I revoke and I renounce every satanic marriage in the dream by the power of the blood of Jesus, in the name of Jesus.**

- **Every demonic wedding ring given to me in the dream, catch fire and burn to ashes ! in the name of Jesus.**

- **If I am being kept from progress because I have been one with a spirit spouse in the dream, blood of Jesus separate me now, in the name of Jesus.**

- **If I am being kept from prosperity because I have become one with a demon through sex in the dream, blood of Jesus separate me now, in the name of Jesus.**

- **If I am being manipulated to enjoy being one with a demon through sex in the dream, blood of Jesus deliver me now, in the name of Jesus.**

- **Power of evil dedication over the 12th month, you shall not steal from me, in the name of Jesus.**

- **I lay the foundation of my desired breakthroughs of the new year on the sacrifice of Christ, in the name of Jesus.**

Reference.
1. DW.Don Whitney's Spiritual Disciplines for the Christian Life

Dictionary of Phrase and Fable, 1894:"Queen

of Heaven with the ancient Phoenicians, was Astarte; Greeks, Hera; Romans, Juno; Trivia, Hecate, Diana, the Egyptian Isis, etc., were all so called; but with the Roman Catholics it is the Virgin Mary."

Ancient Sun Worship and Its Impact on Christianity
By A.T Jones
Extract from "The Two Republics"
Wikipedia: The months of the year.
Margaret Manning: Slice of Infinity Series: Driven to Distraction

E.W Bullinger: Significance of Numbers

Dr. D. K. Olukoya: Smite the enemy and he shall flee!

Each culture of time is backed by its own cosmology.. cosmology is the narrative of creation.
Like us, these folks (hunter-gathers, early farmers or medieval peasants) were schooled in the cosmological vision of their culture. Through rites and rituals, baptisms and burials, people learned the world was built by gods (or

God) and inhabited by devils, demons, divine spirits and watchful angels. Daily time — the round of waking, working and rest — was lived right in the middle of this cosmology. You saw it in the rising sun, the mist on the trees and the stars at night.

Science, when it arrived hundreds of years ago, changed many things. But it didn't alter this braiding of human and cosmic time. When, for example, clocks appeared in 1300 they blew away the old time-logic and set life to a new beat. But their influence went far beyond (and above) daily life. By 1377 the clock as an idea was so powerful that philosopher Nicole Oresme could use it to frame a new cosmology in the image of a clockwork universe. Later, Isaac Newton's science of mechanics was built on this clockwork time, becoming the foundation for a new celestial physics and new real-world machines that set the industrial revolution in motion.http://www.npr.org/blogs/13.7/2011/10/04/141006095/the-end-of-time-as-we-know-it Adam Frank : The end of time as we know it.

...is time the truth as written by the sun, moon and stars?

ABOUT THE AUTHOR

Anthony Akerele is a Geologist by profession and a ministering "Priest and King" at the Mountain of Fire and Miracles Ministries Virginia, in Springfield, Virginia. He is happily married to Nnenna with children. They are both permanently enrolled in the Holy Spirit end time Army.